Western Practice Lessons

Western Practice Lessons

Charlene Strickland

Storey Publishing

The mission of Storey Publishing
is to serve our customers by publishing practical information
that encourages personal independence in harmony with the environment.

Edited by Marie Salter
Copyedited by Dolores York
Cover design by Elizabeth Morrisson
Cover photographs © Gemma Giannini
Text design by Mark Tomasi
Design assistance and production by Susan Bernier
Overhead drawings by Chuck Galey; line drawings by JoAnna Rissanen-Welch;
   helmets on page 7 by James E. Dyekman; Western horse on page 139 by Elayne Sears
Indexed by Susan Olason / Indexes & Knowledge Maps

The information in this book is true and complete to the best of our knowledge. All recommendations are made without guarantee on the part of the author or Storey Publishing. The author and publisher disclaim any liability in connection with the use of this information. For additional information please contact Storey Publishing, 210 MASS MoCA Way, North Adams, MA 01247.

Storey books are available for special premium and promotional uses and for customized editions. For further information, please call 1-800-793-9396.

Printed in China by R.R. Donnelley
10 9 8

Library of Congress Cataloging-in-Publication Data

Strickland, Charlene.
      Western practice lessons / Charlene Strickland.
         p. cm.
      Includes index.
      ISBN-13: 978-158017-107-6;
      ISBN-10: 1-58017-107-9
      1. Western horses — Training.   2. Western riding.
SF309.34 .S76 2000
798.2'3—dc21   99-088041

Contents

Photography Credits viii

Acknowledgments ix

Chapter 1: Introduction 1

Chapter 2: Rhythm 9

Lesson 1 ★ Line through the Lane 10

Lesson 2 ★ Singin' in the Walk 13

Lesson 3 ★ Sit the Jog 16

Lesson 4 ★ Ponderosa Poles 19

Lesson 5 ★ Laredo Lope .22

Summary 25

Chapter 3: Relaxation and Suppleness 27

Lesson 6 ★ In Your Corner 28

Lesson 7 ★ Relax the Jaw .31

Lesson 8 ★ Adjust the Brakes 34

Lesson 9 ★ Sittin' and Bittin' 37

Lesson 10 ★ Idaho Isolation 41

Lesson 11 ★ Break Up the Drive Train 44

Lesson 12 ★ Circle Up 47

Lesson 13 ★ Serpentine Circus 50

Summary 55

Chapter 4: Readiness 57

Lesson 14 ★ Fingertip Controls 58

Lesson 15 ★ Striding and Guiding 61

Lesson 16 ★ Stay on Track 64

Lesson 17 ★ Mirrored Hackamore 68

Lesson 18 ★ Sidepassing 71

Lesson 19 ★ Nevada Neck Rein 74

Lesson 20 ★ Square-Cornered Circles 78

Lesson 21 ★ Refine Your Cues 81

Lesson 22 ★ Boxed In 84

Summary 87

Chapter 5: Impulsion 89

Lesson 23 ★ Turn on the Haunches 90

Lesson 24 ★ Outside Rein Rhythm 94

Lesson 25 ★ Sidewinder 98

Lesson 26 ★ Snake River Serpentines 103

Lesson 27 ★ Coiled Mecate 106

Lesson 28 ★ Dallas Diagonal .109

Lesson 29 ★ Stop on Your Butt 112

Lesson 30 ★ Whirling Walk 115

Summary 117

Chapter 6: Straightness 119

    Lesson 31 ★ Toothpaste Tube 120

    Lesson 32 ★ Albuquerque Jerky .122

    Lesson 33 ★ Forward, Sideways, Back 125

    Lesson 34 ★ Two-Track 129

    Lesson 35 ★ Connected to the Horse 133

    Summary 137

Appendixes 139

    The Western Horse 139

    Further Reading 140

    Associations 141

    Glossary 142

Index 144

Photography Credits

All photographs © by Charlene Strickland, except those by:

★ American Quarter Horse Association on pages i and 2;
★ Giles Prett/Storey Books on pages viii, x, 8, 10, 13, 16, 19, 22, 31, 34, 37, 41, 44, 71, 84, and 106;
★ Galloping Graphics/Susansexton.com on pages 6, 94, 98, and 109; and
★ Gemma Giannini on pages 112 and 138.

Acknowledgments

Thanks to the following trainers for contributing lessons and teachings to this book.

Carolyn Bader, Peralta, New Mexico
   Chapter 3, Lesson 9 ★ Chapter 4, Lesson 15 ★ Chapter 6, Lesson 35

Terry Berg, Santa Fe, New Mexico
   Chapter 4, Lesson 21

Marge Brubaker, Franktown, Colorado
   Chapter 3, Lessons 7, 8, and 10 ★ Chapter 4, Lessons 19 and 22

Gary Ferguson, Temecula, California
   Chapter 3, Lesson 11

Art Gaytan, Burbank, California
   Chapter 5, Lesson 30

Joe and Donna King, City of Industry, California
   Chapter 3, Lesson 6 ★ Chapter 4, Lesson 20

Terry Wegener and Guy Vernon, Kiowa, Colorado
   Chapter 5, Lesson 29

Barbara Keller, Conifer, Colorado

Elsie Anne Shollenbarger, Albuquerque, New Mexico

Storey Publishing extends a special thank you to Carol DeMayo, Lisa DeMayo, and the student riders of DeMayo's Bonnie Lea Farm in Williamstown, Massachusetts, for their assistance.

The discipline of Western riding requires practice. The step-by-step lessons that follow will help you plan, perform, evaluate, and refine your riding, resulting in improved communication between you and your horse.

chapter 1

Introduction

The art of horsemanship assumes many forms, and Western riding is the distinctly American style. When you pull on your cowboy boots and wide-brimmed hat, you celebrate the heritage of the frontier. Sitting deep in the seat of a Western saddle, you link to the traditions of the cowboy. Western riding, unlike the flat saddle disciplines, originated with riders who worked for a living. Cowhands and their speedy Spanish horses herded and roped cattle on the ranches of the Southwest.

Today Western riding is a sport. Riding one of the American breeds, you relish the fun and thrills of a spectrum of Western events, either on the range or in the arena. Horsemanship itself still follows the European traditions of equitation. Cowboys practiced the traditions of Spain's celebrated horsemen, and they patterned their skills on the classic principles. Like the masters of Spain, France, and Italy, they looked for the horse to obey with energy, both in slow, collected gaits and galloping in full extension.

Like any other sport, horsemanship demands practice. Riding is a sequence of events, with the rider guiding the horse toward perfection. The trained horse in any discipline feels light, responsive, and balanced, so he seems to glide gracefully over the ground. At a touch of leg and rein, he bends his body to turn easily. Horse and rider move in harmony.

This book will help you toward this ideal, so you'll have more fun and satisfaction riding your horse. Step-by-step lessons guide you to plan, perform, evaluate, and refine your performance.

These practice lessons lead you through a progression, from simple exercises to more complex patterns. They form a course in Western riding that incorporates a training scale, modified from that used by trainers of Olympic-level dressage horses. The training scale follows these basic concepts:

- Rhythm
- Relaxation and suppleness
- Readiness
- Engagement and impulsion
- Straightness

These concepts are fundamental to riding a broke horse, and the chapters in this book present lessons for each concept. Each chapter builds on its predecessor, with exercises for you to practice. All help you pursue the goal of riding with your horse.

Planning to Learn

These exercises form a foundation for Western riding. By following the lessons, you will:

- Train your horse.
- Feel all facets of your horse's responses.
- Experience variety.
- Gain satisfaction through a greater involvement with your horse.
- Prepare to meet show requirements for specific tests in equitation, horsemanship, and trail.

Lessons structure the way you train your horse. By following a training scale, lessons give you goals. You'll ride like a trainer, with objectives for the lessons you teach your horse. Think of lessons as quality time that you spend with your horse. You ride purposefully, and you dictate your riding time.

Riding involves thinking and feeling. To become a horseman, you act as a thinking athlete. You think through every movement to figure out what works for you and your horse. If your horse makes a mistake, examine what you did or did not tell him. You also focus on feeling what you do, how your horse responds, and then deciding what to do next. Repeating these lessons imprints a feel of proper techniques into your mind and body. You are never just a passenger but the leading partner in a dance of two creatures.

You want to look like a rider who performs with smoothness, accuracy, and thoughtfulness. To onlookers, you may appear to do nothing — yet you are constantly communicating with your horse.

Improving Your Horse

Every ride is a learning opportunity for you and a training opportunity for your horse. You either school your horse to improve, or allow him to lapse into a bad habit. First, every horse needs to know these basics:

- Walk, turn, and "whoa"
- Jog, turn, and "whoa"
- Lope, turn, and "whoa"
- Back up

Partner with your horse as you practice your Western riding skills in this progression of lessons. The results will help you in the show ring and beyond.

You can practice these lessons on any horse, pony, or mule that knows these basics, or on a well-trained, finished horse. (No horse is absolutely perfect.) If your horse is green, you'll probably stick with the first two chapters for a while. You want to aim for consistency before you step up the demands. The lessons in chapters 5 and 6 will be more satisfying on a well-schooled horse. The exercises and patterns in the lessons will improve your horse's performance. You can make a mediocre horse perform better through training.

In the process of improving the horse, you'll also advance in your riding skills. You'll be on the way to becoming a "good hand" with a horse. These lessons aren't meant to teach you to sit pretty — rather, the steps help you facilitate the horse's responses.

Better riding leads to a better horse. Your horse reflects your riding because riding is a sequence of actions and reactions. These lessons help your horse to learn these positive habits:

- Obedience
- Listening
- Flexing and bending
- Adjustment
- Elasticity and suppleness
- Staying on the track

Moving up the scale should present you and your horse with greater challenges. You'll build on the basics, guiding the horse's impulsion to lengthen and shorten his strides. To go forward, impulsion generates extension. To come back, impulsion contributes to collection.

Coaching Yourself

Lessons help you maintain discipline. They give you short-term objectives that you can achieve and long-term goals you seek to perfect.

You may already take regular lessons from an instructor, who acts as your mentor. You can use these lessons in addition to instruction to practice the concepts you learn in class. You can keep yourself motivated on the days you're on your own.

Mental Fitness

You'll act as your own coach in these lessons. Self-coaching does require certain mental attributes, beginning with your faith in your ability to improve yourself and your horse.

Confident. You know that you're proficient in your riding skills. You're able to control your body so you can positively influence your horse. You sit erect in the saddle and ride in balance with your horse. You're able to relax enough so you don't cause your horse to move stiffly or tensely.

Horsewise. You learn to recognize what's right, and what's not right, in your horse's behavior. You tune into your horse to understand why he responds the way he does. You know what to ask, and when to ask — when to push, and when to leave alone. You learn to think ahead of your horse.

Patient. You can remain cool, whatever your horse does. You ride without expressing emotion. Wait for the breakthroughs, and they will come.

Determined. You analyze your horse's response and carry on, regardless of problems or setbacks. Affirm your ultimate aims, and be ready to conquer any roadblocks to your success. Ideally your horse's personality should match with yours — if not, you persist in guiding his actions. Don't despair — if you really want to ride better, persevere!

Blame-free. You don't blame the horse, and you don't make excuses. You accept the occasional failure without accusations.

Goals

Every coach sets goals. To coach yourself, you become self-motivated and self-directed.

Set your game plan, with major goals you want to achieve. Clearly define what you want to achieve with this horse and how you will benefit from achieving your goals. Stick to your goals by mapping out your plan. On a white board or wall calendar, write down goals by the month, quarter, or year. Plan how many times a week you can ride, and how many days will be lesson days.

 Ringside Reference

Place this book in a plastic cookbook holder. Set the holder on a fence rail, table, or chair beside your riding area. If you want to carry a lesson with you, photocopy the pages in reduced size and tuck them in your shirt pocket or fanny pack.

Honesty

Coaching yourself means you pay attention to what you and your horse do. Imagine an instructor in the middle of your ring or schooling area. That person watches every move you make and can read every thought in your mind. She tells you what to do, how you do it, and how you should be doing it.

You play both roles: the constantly talking (sometimes nagging!) teacher and the eager student. A teacher evaluates, and the student adjusts. Listen to yourself, the teacher. Check your position at each gait — head, shoulders, back, seat, hands, heels. When you make a turn or transition, mentally observe each part of your body and how your horse reacts. Has your position shifted? Is your horse correct? Fix it before your teacher mentions it!

Are you sitting crooked or uneven in any way? Did you remember to work both sides of your horse equally, or did you school a bit longer on his weaker side today?

Balanced Progress

Each lesson contains learning objectives to help you monitor your progress. While wearing your "teacher's hat," measure your results against the objectives. Then, back as the student, adjust your lessons to improve your performance. Concentrate on what you find difficult. Sticking to easy routines can be satisfying, but you'll accomplish more when you confront what's tougher for you.

Remember to balance schooling with relaxed work. Learn when you should be satisfied and when to stop asking your horse. Although you're persistent, you need to learn to let go. Don't bore your horse by drilling him on the same maneuvers or patterns. Even though Western riding follows a horse's natural movements, realize that the horse wouldn't repeat them as much as you might. Avoid overdoing a step or lesson, and don't ride like a fanatic.

As you teach your horse, look for the "aha." Recognize that moment of success, and stop to praise him and savor the occasion. You want to reward a positive reaction that's been a long time coming.

Using This Book

To learn from a book, you read, look, and imitate. This workbook contains structured lessons that are recipes for better horsemanship. In addition to the steps you follow in the saddle, each lesson includes the sections outlined in the box below.

Lessons also include **Tips** and **Horse Sense,** things to watch for to help you avoid common errors. Some lessons add **Focus on Form,** a snapshot of a moment that you compare to your own horsemanship.

Optional **Challenge** segments offer variations to increase the degree of difficulty. Some lessons also suggest alternate approaches that you may practice.

Objectives	Every lesson has learning objectives that show you what you'll be able to do as a result of the lesson.
Benefits	The lesson can improve the horse in certain ways. Benefits list the value of the lesson.
Suggested time frame of short, medium, or long	You may have time for a short lesson of 10–15 minutes. Or, try combining a short and medium lesson into a full 30–45 minutes. A long lesson runs about 40 minutes. Remember that professional trainers ride colts from 30–60 minutes a day, five days a week.
Setup (preparation)	You may need to arrange markers, such as cones or barrels, in your riding area. Some lessons specify riding in a fenced pen. (Not all lessons need specific setup.)

Key to Arena Illustrations

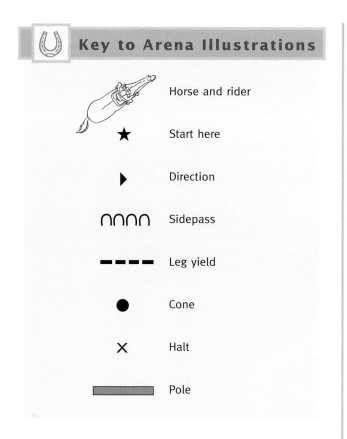

Horse and rider

★   Start here

▶   Direction

∩∩∩∩   Sidepass

▬ ▬ ▬ ▬   Leg yield

●   Cone

✕   Halt

▭   Pole

More complex lessons are divided into parts. You can practice a pattern and then take a break. Let your horse settle in a free walk or stand still, while you evaluate your success. Reflect on what you've accomplished, and ask yourself, "Am I able to reach the results I seek? How well do I meet the standards of the ideal performance?"

Most of the lessons assume that you're riding two-handed, with a snaffle bit. You can increase the challenge in any lesson by switching to a curb bit and riding one-handed.

You can follow a lesson in different ways, according to your personal learning style. When riding by yourself, read a lesson before you mount up to practice. Map out your moves by drawing a miniature arena, and use a model horse to practice before your ride.

For safety, you should always ride with at least one other person in the vicinity. A ringside helper, such as a friend or parent, can act as your ground person in or alongside the pen. Ask this assistant to read lesson steps to you while you practice. This person might also agree to record your lessons, using a still camera at each step or a video recorder for lesson segments.

Even better, train with at least one other rider. In a group lesson, you and a fellow rider can help talk each other through the steps. If you ride in a threesome or more, your group can even stage a practice show to test everyone's skills.

After a lesson, do an honest critique. Listen to your assistant or fellow riders, and accept their opinions as constructive criticism. Study photos or videos — make notes on how you'll revise your training sessions to concentrate on problems. You can then critique yourself again in a week or a month to see where you've improved.

Adapt these lessons to your horse's personality and your own ideas. Make up new figures, or even go through the steps backward. Challenge when challenge is needed.

This book includes horsemen's terms in the lessons, all of which are defined in the glossary that begins on page 142. You'll also find a list of associations and suggestions for other helpful books.

Preparing for Lessons

Before practicing, follow a preride checklist. Your "flight plan" will ensure the safety of both you and your horse.

You may choose to wear spurs or carry a whip, depending on your horse's attitude. If he ignores or resists your cues, you need to respond with a similar insistence. You should never abuse your horse, but always make your cue equal to his resistance.

Western riders train with the snaffle bit, riding two-handed. This style trains the horse to follow his nose and keep his shoulders lifted. You can still neck-rein your horse, and you can switch to the curb bit to increase the challenge, as noted in "Using This Book" on page 4.

Preride Checklist

★ **Horse**   Clean, sound, and healthy, with shod or trimmed feet

★ **Tack**   Saddle correctly fitted and adjusted, cinched above a clean saddle pad

★ **Bridle**   Headstall and reins with a snaffle bit, correctly adjusted

★ **Attire**   Boots or riding sneakers, long pants, riding helmet

In the practice pen, you'll "ride the range" on your Western horse. Markers like these cones help you ride through patterns.

Location

Choose a safe site for your practice lessons. Unless you're riding a very green horse, you don't need to stay within an enclosed arena or round pen. Look for safe footing, ideally flat and appropriate to the speed you'll ride. If the ground's muddy or slick, you can still ride, provided you stay at a walk or slow jog.

Props

Props do help you practice. You can use logs, wooden fence posts, or jump poles to form lanes or low obstacles to walk, jog, or lope over. For practicing turns, you'll arrange barrels, cones, or jump standards. Or, you can maneuver your horse around natural obstacles such as trees, bushes, or boulders. Any portable or permanent markers will help you focus on direction and precision.

Warm Up

Before you begin a lesson, warm up yourself and your horse. Loosen up your body with stretching exercises as you walk your horse in a large circle. Touch your hand to toe, both on the same side and the opposite side. (If your horse isn't used to your leaning over, do your stretching before you mount.)

Attitude

Test your horse's mental attitude by jogging in a straight line for 20 strides, then asking for a halt. In less than a minute, you can see what sort of equine attitude you're dealing with that day. Is the horse willing to jog or ready to trot right out? How readily does he respond to "whoa"? From this initial response, you'll gauge how much more warm-up you'll need to do before the two of you are ready to tackle a lesson.

 Use Your Head!

Every time you ride a horse, wear a helmet. Not all helmets offer adequate protection. Be sure to buy one that is ASTM/SEI approved. An appropriately sized helmet is comfortable and fits snugly on your head. Many styles are available, the standard equestrian safety helmet and a Western style among them. Unfortunately, many Western riders resist wearing head protection, which can result in needless harm and injury. Use your head each time you ride by protecting it.

Equestrian safety helmet

Western-style helmet

Examine your own attitude, too. To communicate successfully with your horse, approach riding in a positive mental state. You're going to concentrate on what you do and how your horse "answers" you. Clear your mind of other human concerns — you must control yourself first, before you can control your horse. You'll be thinking for the two of you!

Maintain an alert attitude and regular cadence at the walk, jog, and lope.

chapter 2
Rhythm

To cover ground, the horse walks, jogs, and lopes. Every gait has its own rhythm, and the confident horse moves in balance. The broke horse moves in a consistent rhythm with a confirmed cadence.

Whether you ride the trail or go for the Open Reining in Oklahoma City, you help the horse sustain balance and grace. He performs each gait in rhythm according to your guidance. To help your horse, you will control your body to control your horse. Your body weight can change a gait's rhythm. You sit with the motion, ahead of the motion, or behind the motion at every footfall.

Maintaining rhythmic motion requires a feel for each gait. But before you can help your horse's rhythm, you need to understand his individual sequence of hoofbeats. Watch your horse at liberty and on the longe line — how he goes forward willingly, without weight on his back.

How does he move into each gait, and what rhythm seems most natural and comfortable? Study his top line (spine), and watch the hind leg closest to you. At the walk and trot, you should see each hind foot overstep (step over) the print made by the front foot on the same side. If you can't see this in motion, have a helper lead your horse over a damp or wet piece of ground, at the walk and trot. Look at the hoofprints to see the amount of overstep. At the lope, the horse should reach his inside hind foot far forward, under the cantle of your saddle.

Listen to the footfalls. When you ride, you'll aim to duplicate the natural movement that you see and hear. You will train your horse to improve his movement, to be more in rhythm and cadence. He'll move freely forward at a comfortable speed. Recognize what speed is normal for him — it's better to have a horse smooth and slightly fast rather than too slow, shuffling, and not regular in his gaits.

Watch your horse. The way he holds his head, neck, and tail indicates his balance. He should breathe regularly, and his tail should swing as his hind legs come underneath his body. Look for him to float across the ground with a relaxed back. Tension in the back shows in the neck and the tail.

These lessons will help you "conduct" your horse's rhythm. You'll help your horse move more comfortably as you feel and ride with his natural way of going. You'll also learn to tune into your horse's attitude. He must respond to you in his mind before he changes his gait. Look for a quiet attitude, with your horse acknowledging your cues. If he is too lazy or tense, he will not be willing to move where and how you want.

FOOTFALLS OF REGULAR RHYTHM

Gait	Footfall	Description
Walk	1, 2, 3, 4	Ground-covering, alert
Jog	1, 2	Two distinct beats
Lope	1, 2, 3	Rolling, 3-beat rhythm: daaa, dum, dum

Line through the Lane

Eyes front, you ride your horse in a steady rhythm in a straight line. The action seems simple, but horses tend to wander. To guide a horse in this basic exercise requires you to stay alert to each footfall's tempo and direction. You'll feel more comfortable sitting on your horse as you tune in and pay attention to his strides.

At any gait, keep your horse's rhythm in a straight line.

Objectives

- To keep your horse's rhythm on a straight line
- To use your aids to help your horse maintain rhythm
- To keep your horse walking straight, with his neck bent to the inside, then to the outside

Benefits

- Every horse must move forward at a constant rate and in a steady direction.
- This lesson will especially benefit the young or green horse, and it will help you feel easy in your seat.

Time Frame — Short

Setup

A flat place with footing of slightly soft or damp dirt, at least 60 feet (20 m) in length, not too close to a fence or wall

On the dirt, drive a car, truck, or tractor in a straight line for at least 60 feet (20 m). The tire tracks will form the lane you'll use in this lesson. If you don't have access to a vehicle, draw two parallel lines in the dirt, about 6 feet (2 m) apart.

Step-by-Step

1. Walk to the beginning of your lane and cue your horse to halt. Say "whoa," **sit deep, pull reins softly, and release rein pressure.** Feel how your horse answered your request. Was he willing or reluctant? ▶

2. **Stand up in the stirrups, and reach forward to touch the horse's neck.** ▶

3. Put your hands on the saddle horn. Still standing, look down at your legs. Are your feet directly under you? You may feel more comfortable with your toes positioned just ahead of your knees.

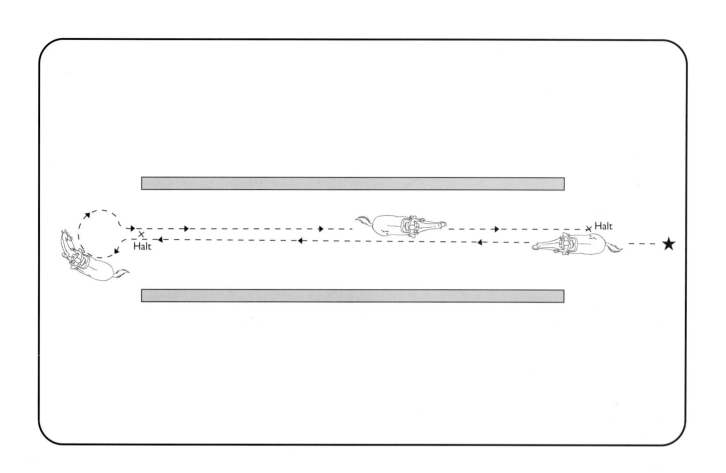

Step 1:
Sit deep, pull reins softly, and release rein pressure.

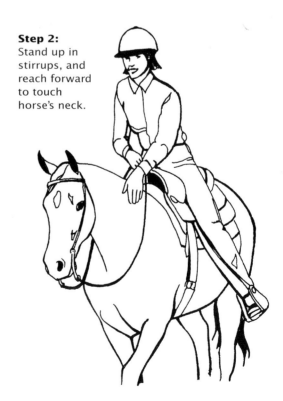

Step 2:
Stand up in stirrups, and reach forward to touch horse's neck.

4. Settle back down in the saddle, and hold your reins in your left hand.

5. Reach down with your right hand and touch your knee, thigh, and toe. Keep your balance by pressing down in your left stirrup.

6. Sit up, and switch the reins to your right hand. Reach down with your left hand and touch your knee, thigh, and toe. Keep your balance by pressing down in your right stirrup.

7. Sit up, and wiggle your seat into the saddle. Hold the reins in both hands, about 6 inches (15 cm) apart.

8. Ask for a crisp walk. Squeeze with both legs to urge the horse forward. Feel your horse's willingness to respond.

9. Walk on a straight line in the lane. Listen to the walk. Do you hear the steady rhythm, 1, 2, 3, 4? Feel how you move with the horse.

10. With your right rein, tip the horse's nose to the right. Pull softly straight back (using the direct rein) to bend his neck slowly to the right, still walking forward.

    Change the bend gradually without changing cadence, and stay in your lane at the same pace. You may have to squeeze with your legs if your horse slows rhythm.

11. Maintain the bend for four strides.

12. Gradually straighten the horse so he moves straight for eight strides.

13. Repeat the bend in Steps 10 and 11 to the left.

14. **Straighten and continue walking** to the end of the lane. ▶

15. Halt at the end of the lane. Say "whoa" and sit deep. If the horse doesn't stop, bump him with the reins and release.

16. Stand in place while you count to ten.

17. Resume the walk, beyond the lane, and do a half-circle to change direction.

18. Repeat the exercise going in the opposite direction.

Tips

- Did your horse respond to what you asked? Did he move out at a lively, deliberate walk?
- Did you remain in balance?
- Did your hands and legs remain steady? Did your heels come up as you bent the horse?
- Did you slowly apply the rein to ask for the bend?
- Did you move the least amount necessary to control the horse?

Horse Sense

- Ask your horse to walk, then tell him to walk if he drags his toes in a lazy manner.

  You may need to kick your horse if he's too slow. Make your correction obvious, with a definite kick behind the girth, and wait for the response. If you can't tell he did anything, he's ignoring you. Kick again, harder.
- Many horses tend to drift. Try to keep his feet in the center of your lane.
- Correct your horse carefully — not too abruptly, and not too little.
- Watch for your horse to change his rhythm as you start to bend him.
- As you make the circle at the end of the lane, your horse might speed up going "toward the gate.

Step 14: Straighten and continue walking.

Singin' in the Walk

You've got the beat, and your music can match the strides of your horse's walk. Don't think that walking is boring, because an active, four-beat walk is the foundation of the other gaits. The tempo you sing or chant sends your horse forward, one step at a time. Eyes up, shoulders back, and heels down . . . march!

Objectives

- To maintain an energetic, rhythmic walk
- To encourage your horse to step out at a comfortable walk
- To apply the alternating leg aids to achieve a ground-covering walk with more overstep

Benefit

The walk is the foundation gait for any Western horse. Every horse must walk freely in a consistent cadence.

Time Frame — Short

Setup

Learn the tune and words to a good walking song. The song should match your horse's walk. The tempo should "march" with a 1–2 beat so you can emphasize every other syllable as you sing while you walk your horse. You don't have to sing the actual words. A few suggestions:

- The theme from "Jeopardy" (da, *da,* da, *da,* da, *da,* da . . .)
- "If I Fell" (Beatles)
- "Out of Time" (Rolling Stones)

You can practice this lesson anywhere. You may want to ride by yourself, as others may wonder why you're singing to your horse.

Direct your horse in the four-beat walk, tuning in to his regular rhythm.

Step-by-Step

1. Signal your horse to walk out.

2. Glance down at his left shoulder. As you see it move forward in a stride, sing the first syllable of your song. ▼

Step 2

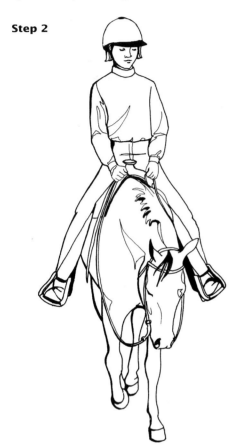

3. Sing the second beat to correspond with the second stride of his left shoulder. You'll sing the emphasized syllable to syncopate with his left shoulder. The unemphasized syllables match the strides of his right shoulder.

4. Continue to sing. Halt after two verses. If your riding area isn't long enough to complete both verses in a straight line, guide your horse into a wide, sweeping turn or circle.

   Ask yourself if your horse kept up with the beats. If you're not sure, repeat two verses of your song and halt.

5. Resume the walk. Feel your seat in the saddle, moving with the horse's steps.

6. Glance down at the horse's left shoulder. As he strides forward, **press your right heel against his barrel,** behind the cinch. ▼

Step 6

Focus on Form

Sit in the middle of the horse. Line up your navel with the saddle horn and neck of the horse. Keep your heels level or down, pointing your toes slightly up. Your legs should stay under you, not swinging forward or back. The lower parts of your legs should be close to your horse. If you ride in horsemanship classes, you'd want to sit straight so an imaginary vertical line runs from your ear down to your heel. Move with the horse, without an exaggerated motion. Hold the reins with wrists straight so you form a straight line from your elbow to the horse's mouth.

7. As he strides with the right shoulder, press your left heel against his barrel.

8. Continue using the alternating leg for at least 20 strides, or 40 presses.

9. Halt and pet your horse.

Horse Sense

Your horse might speed up, so be sure to adjust your leg cues to his response.

Challenge

Combine your song with the alternating leg, so you sing and squeeze at the same moment.

 Leg Cues

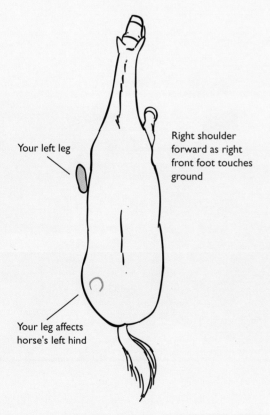

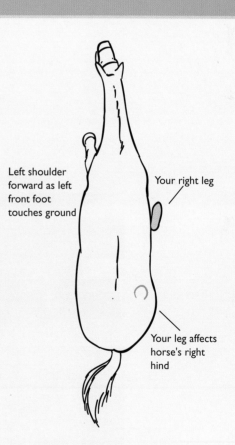

In the alternating leg, adjust the amount of pressure to your horse's response. Pressing too lightly or too hard will result in no response or too much speeding up. You want to feel your horse extend his stride, not walk more rapidly.

The alternating leg influences the forward stride of the horse's hind leg on the same side that you press. As the left shoulder goes forward, you press your right leg. You are influencing the horse's right hind leg.

Sit the Jog

Count out, "1-2, 1-2." Whether you ride in a Western or flat saddle, your hips absorb the trot steps. Cowhands sit the slow jog trot, easing comfortably in the saddle. Like them, you'll learn to sit the balanced movement with the horse's motion. Loosen up those shock absorbers!

Objectives

- To maintain the horse's rhythm at the jog
- To attain and maintain cadence till you say stop
- To ride with the motion of the horse, sitting deep and feeling his movement

Benefits

- Western riding uses the jog trot, especially in shows. Both you and the horse have to be comfortable at this gait.
- You will influence the horse to maintain rhythm and cadence.
- You will start to learn about your horse's natural energy. Is he lazy or hot?

Time Frame — Short

Setup

Enclosed area, such as round pen, small corral, arena

Feel the rhythm of the horse's diagonal movement at the jog.

16

Step-by-Step

1. Sit in the middle of the horse, over his balance point (center of gravity). Let your hips sit deep, and feel the horse's sides with your calves. ▼

Step 1

2. Squeeze with your calves to move the horse into a jog straight ahead. (If you're in a round pen or small corral, you'll jog in a circle.)

3. Feel the horse move into a rhythm. Count the cadence: 1-2, 1-2. Pick up his rhythm as you absorb the shock during a steady gait. Feel the forward motion of the near hind leg, and feel the subsequent footfalls with your seatbones.

4. After you've jogged about ten strides, **close your eyes** to immerse yourself into the feeling. **Feel the shifts of the horse's weight,** right-left, right-left. Hold onto the saddle horn if you feel unsteady.

Do you feel you're still in the middle? Have you moved ahead of or behind the rhythm? Did the horse move you ahead or behind? If so, tip your body back or forward by bending at the waist. ▶

Tips

■ Feel that you and your horse move spine to spine, with your hips moving sideways with the rhythm: left-right, left-right. Don't bounce up and down or "fight" the motion. Think of your abdomen as "jelly belly."

■ Take a mental snapshot every few strides to check your position. You should remain in the middle of the horse, sitting tall. You're not fighting your horse, but you're also not allowing him to shift your weight forward or back.

■ If you have an assistant watching you, ask her to tell you when the horse's hind leg pushes from the ground.

■ You may speak to your horse, but think mostly about the tone of your voice. (Horses don't understand English.) Say quiet words softly: "whoa," "easy." Say correction words more sharply: "quit," "hup."

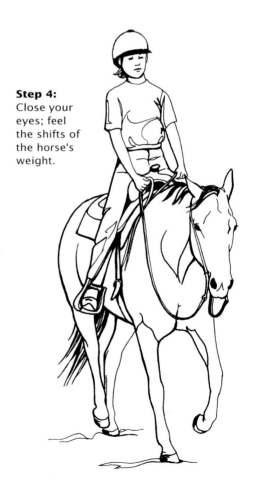

Step 4: Close your eyes; feel the shifts of the horse's weight.

5. Open your eyes and see what you're feeling. Jog 20 strides, and feel for the motion of the inside hind leg. Can you feel the horse place that foot and then push off the ground?

Be aware of your jaw. Do you clench your jaw and tense your chin and lips? Count out loud, "1-2, 1-2."

6. Sit down, even deeper, and halt. How did the horse respond to your cue? Did he listen to you, and was he sensitive to your signal? Did he start to slow as you asked for the halt? ▼

Step 6

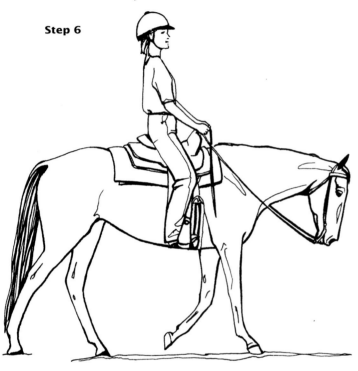

7. Count to 10, slowly.

8. Walk your horse across the enclosed area.

9. Repeat Steps 2 through 6, going in the opposite direction.

Feel the horse's cadence. You should feel as if he's marching. Is his gait consistent, the same at the first stride as the last? Or does he slow his tempo, or speed up?

10. Halt and pet your horse.

Focus on Form

- Let your hips move with the saddle. If the seat pushes you up, you still experience contact with the saddle.
- Try to keep your heels down. First point your toes up, and then put weight into the balls of your feet and put your heels down. Stand up to stretch, and sink back down.

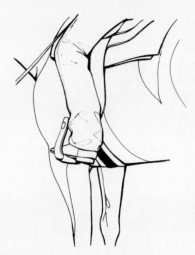

- Your legs shouldn't move back and forth. Drop one stirrup, and raise your knee toward the pommel. Hold it for a few strides, then switch to the other knee.
- Hold the reins with your thumbs up. Think of holding an ice cream cone.
- Smile and breathe.

Horse Sense

- Your horse might become bored and slow down. Influence the movement when his near hind leg is on the ground. Squeeze with your inside calf.
- The horse could speed up. Check him with a bump of the reins, and release. Don't hang on the reins.

Challenge

- Keep your eyes closed during the entire exercise.
- Test your horse. Think "whoa," and see if he stops.

lesson 4

Ponderosa Poles

Here's the first lesson using props. You'll steer your horse across poles or rails, laid flat on the ground. Even if you'll never show in a trail class, walking over poles helps your horse find his rhythm. He'll pay attention to your guidance because you set the tempo, speed, and direction. He'll also increase his trust in your cues to pick up his feet and keep moving forward.

Objectives

- To practice crisp transitions from the walk to the jog and the jog to the walk
- To improve your horse's obedience in the upward and downward transitions
- To reach and keep a regular rhythm at the walk and the jog

Benefits

- Your horse will listen to you while he watches his footing over the poles, and you will start listening to your horse more when you cue him.
- The horse will learn to relax his back and neck as he jogs over the poles.
- The horse will travel calmly over low obstacles, in balance.
- This exercise is basic to preparing horse and rider for Trail and Western Riding classes.

Time Frame — Medium

Setup

You will need at least four poles. Place the first one on the ground, with the others close by to add later.

Walking over poles helps you concentrate on maintaining your horse's rhythm.

Step-by-Step

Single Pole

1. Walk your horse toward the pole on the ground, aiming his nose at the middle of the pole.

2. **Tip your body slightly forward** as he lifts his feet to walk over the pole. ▶

3. When all four feet are on the opposite side of the pole, sit back down and ask for the jog.

4. Jog a half-circle.

5. Aim your horse at the pole.

6. As he nears the pole, tip your body slightly forward as he lifts his feet to jog over the pole.

7. After he crosses the pole with all four feet, slow to a walk.

8. Watch your horse's ears, and ask for the halt. Did he swivel his ears back to you? Did he keep his ears forward or lay them back in resentment?

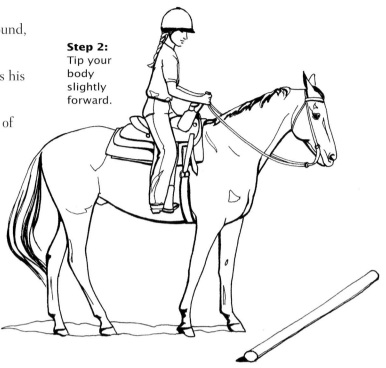

Step 2: Tip your body slightly forward.

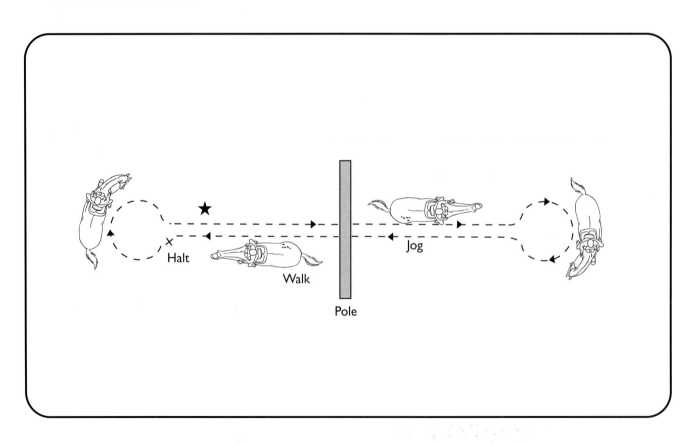

Halt · Walk · Pole · Jog

9. Walk a half-circle.

10. Repeat Steps 1 through 7. Watch his ears throughout, so you see his attitude toward you and the exercise.

11. Halt and pet your horse.

Two Poles

1. Add Pole 2, about 6 feet (2 m) from Pole 1.

2. Walk over both poles, and feel how your horse handles the distance between them. If he has to stretch or compress his stride, change the spacing between poles. You want the horse to walk a comfortable stride between the poles. ▶

3. Repeat the transitions of the Single Pole.

. . . And More Poles

Repeat the exercise, adding Poles 3 and 4.

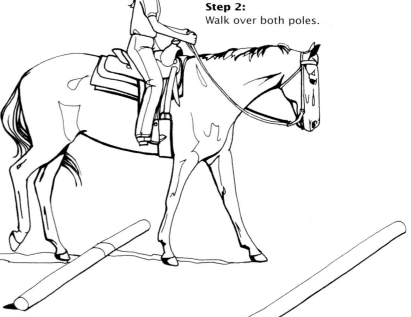

Step 2:
Walk over both poles.

Tips

▪ Approach calmly and confidently. Look ahead, not down.
▪ Your horse may slow his rhythm as he nears the pole. Squeeze to keep him moving forward in the same cadence.
▪ Ride "light" to help your horse.
▪ Keep with the motion as you walk and jog, and don't let your hand jerk the horse's mouth.
▪ Keep a consistent contact with your calves.
▪ Build your horse's confidence. Listen to how he feels when he first approaches the single pole. If he wobbles in the approach, squeeze him forward and cluck to him.

Horse Sense

▪ Don't change your position as you change gait.
▪ Your horse should not step on or kick a pole.

 Focus on Form

Look where you're going. Your leg position should not change. When you jog over a pole, stand up in the stirrups for a stride before and after.

Challenge

▪ Jog the entire exercise.
▪ Start your jog from a halt, with no walk steps.
▪ When you ask for the halt, allow the horse a few walk steps in the downward transition.

Laredo Lope

The lope challenges many horses. If yours is lazy, he could lose that 1-2-3 rhythm. A hot horse can resist that easygoing gait and spurt forward into a gallop. On your way to Laredo, look for smooth upward (jog to lope) and downward (lope to jog) transitions. And you'll also start to lope where you look.

Objectives

- To establish rhythm at the lope
- To achieve a crisp transition into the lope
- To improve your seat at the lope

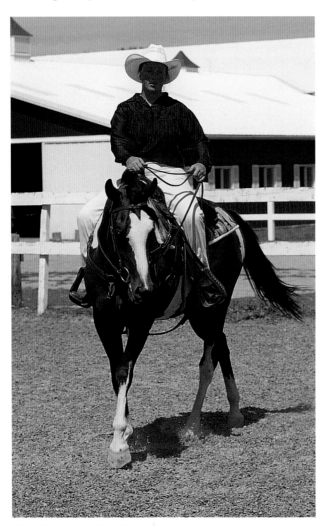

Your horse drives forward at the lope, on turns, and in a straight line.

Benefits

- A steady, three-beat lope is important to every Western horse. Your horse needs to maintain his balance in the upward and downward transitions.
- You will gain confidence by controlling your horse at the lope.

Time Frame — Short

Setup — Enclosed arena

Step-by-Step

1. Move your horse into a jog, forming the first leg of the **L** for Laredo.

2. After ten strides at a steady rhythm, visualize your horse stepping off into the lope. **Look to the left.** ▼

Step 2

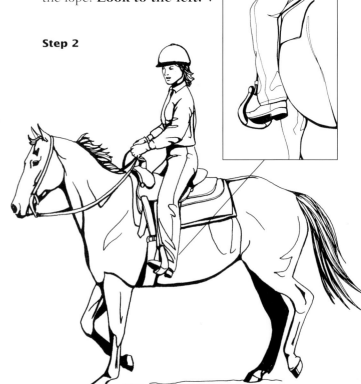

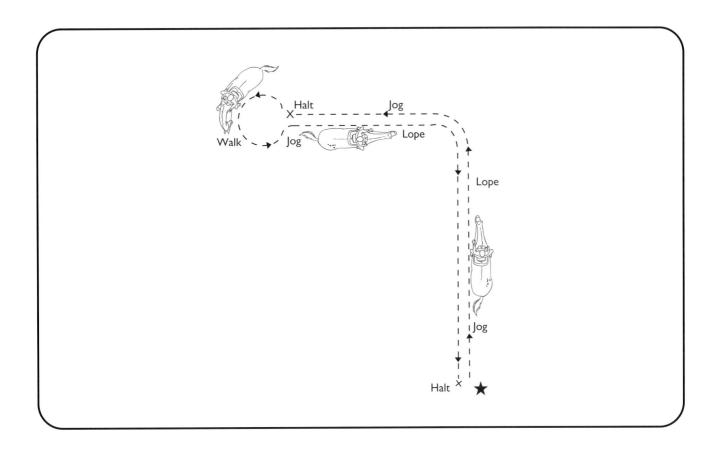

3. Give the signals for the lope on the left lead. On most horses, you will feel the left rein and squeeze with the right leg. You may need to cluck or "kiss" to the horse.

Feel what happens under you, as the horse gathers his legs for the transition. Which hind leg starts to move forward first? Can you feel the thrust in the departure?

4. Lope straight ahead for ten strides. Sit deep and absorb the motion. Does your horse lope steady, so you can feel and hear the three beats? Many horses don't. You may have to ask him to speed up or slow down. If you hear four beats, squeeze with both legs and cluck so the horse moves forward at a slightly faster gait.

Feel your horse lift his back as he drives forward with the inside hind leg.

5. Rein the horse into a wide, sweeping turn. You will form the second leg of the **L** for Laredo. ▶

Step 5:
Rein the horse into a wide, sweeping turn.

6. Sit deeper, with your lower leg "long," and signal the horse to jog for five strides. In this downward transition from lope to jog, you want to sit without moving.

7. Signal your horse to halt, and pet him.

8. Count to 20.

9. Walk your horse on a half-circle to the left.

10. Going in the opposite direction, pick up the jog.

11. Repeat Steps 2 through 7. See if you can lighten your cues for the upward and downward transitions. Are the figures the same size and shape as you made them in the first round?

Tips

- If your horse starts on the wrong lead, stop him and signal again.
- The horse may lope too fast. Stop, count to ten, and cue again for the lope. Don't squeeze as hard with your leg.
- The horse may trot faster instead of loping. Slow him to a walk, and cue from the walk. Be definite in your signal. When you tell him to lope, he answers "Yes" and lopes.
- Your horse could be too lazy. Make him work until you say stop.
- Does your horse lope too slowly, so he feels as if he's laboring every stride? If so, he's likely to use his head and neck to propel himself, and he can "fall on the forehand" or get "strung out" behind. Squeeze with your calves to urge the horse forward, so he feels lighter in front.

Horse Sense

- Don't "rock" into the lope. Keep your heels down and sit deep.
- Don't rein sharply into the turn of the L.
- Watch that you don't pull your horse into the halt. Squeeze with your calves as you signal with "whoa" and pick up contact on the reins. Give when your horse responds.

Challenge

- Reduce the pressure of your cues to move your horse out and slow him down. Try a squeeze of the calf and a nudge of the heel to pick up the lope. Ask for the downward transitions with your voice.
- Pick up the lope from a walk.
- Pick up the lope from a standstill.
- As you lope, close your eyes for three strides. Can you feel the sequence of footfalls?

 Focus on Form

Sit deep and heavy. Let your hip follow the motion of the horse, but don't wiggle from side to side. Any movement should be forward and back, without your seat slapping the saddle.

You'll always affect your horse's rhythm. All your riding builds on this basic element of correct forward movement. Think about these elements of your horse's rhythm:

Regularity. Consistent footfalls in measured cadence.

Energy. Willing forward movement, with the power to propel.

Obedience. Responsive to your leg, seat, and hands.

Relaxation. Back, neck, and tail feel loose and free, swinging with the gait and breathing regularly.

Think about how you ride these lessons:

Confidence. You feel assured about guiding your horse. You keep him working so every lap is the same, and you expect better when you repeat an exercise.

Position. You sit steady and quiet in the saddle. You maintain a consistent contact with the saddle and sit in the middle of the horse.

Cues. You maintain a steady forward pace, making a difference rather than simply sitting still.

 Use Your Head!

Every time you ride a horse, wear a helmet. Many Western riders resist wearing head protection, which can result in needless harm and injury. Use your head each time you ride by protecting it.

Planning. Set your horse up for any transition. One or two strides before you change direction or gait, think about what response you expect. Cue your horse for that response, then check how he reacts. If he resists — by not paying attention or by telling you "No" — correct him.

The lessons in chapter 3 will further develop your horse's rhythm, as you improve the suppleness of his body.

A horse sensitive to your signals responds more easily, with a relaxed attitude and supple body.

chapter 3

Relaxation and Suppleness

The lessons in chapter 2 helped you ride your horse forward and actively. Now you will practice exercises to help him learn to relax and give to your signals. You will think "lightness" as your goal in these lessons: light to the leg, light to the hand.

You'll observe your horse for feedback on your skill. You will use your leg and seat as signals, and you will expect him to understand your signals.

Your horse is constantly "talking" to you. You look, listen, and feel for certain responses to what he "says." What you want to feel is your horse giving to pressure. Your signals of reins, legs, and weight apply and release pressure so you bend and flex the horse both longitudinally and laterally.

As you watch horses move and ride their movements, you understand the limits of the horse's body. A horse's rigid spine prevents him from demonstrating the flexion of a cat, but the best horses move in a catlike manner. When you ride your horse, pay attention to his physical ability.

If he understands and doesn't respond, ask yourself why. Is this because your horse can't or won't respond? He might be uncomfortable in a certain

movement. He could lack the scope to turn or move as quickly as you want, or he could be in pain from more strenuous motions. Or, he could have a resistant mental attitude.

Helping your horse become more supple will make him a better riding horse. You will help him perform in balance through cooperation. Bending and flexing exercises can improve a horse that tends to be clumsy. Bending the horse also affirms your control. (The horse has to have his spine aligned — straight from neck to tail — before he can rear or buck.)

Don't forget that your horse feels what you think. Your body changes to express your emotions. Your horse feels when your breathing changes, your heart beats faster, or you're upset. He also perceives when you're confident and pleased. You show him the way by channeling your emotions.

Always remember to look for a response. Recognize a correct reaction to your signals, and quit asking when your horse responds correctly. You look for a steady, consistent performance, and you reward him for behaving as you want.

In Your Corner

Before you can expect your horse's body to relax and become supple, you'll ask him to yield his jaw. A tense jaw and tight chin prevent the rest of the body from coming "through" to move where you want. Resistance begins in the jaw, as your horse "sets his mind" to evade your request. California trainer Joe King recommends this standing-in-place exercise as a basic step for any Western horse.

Reins and legs ask the horse to yield. Hold the reins and bump with your legs.

Objectives

- To help your horse become sensitive to your legs
- To touch your horse with your legs so he drops his head and neck
- To control the horse's body by controlling his head position

Benefits

- You will not pull with the reins to ask the horse to give his head to you.
- You will stay off the horse's mouth.
- Your horse will understand to drop his head with your legs, and he will have a light mouth.

Time Frame — Short

Setup

A pen where two fences meet at a 90-degree angle

Step-by-Step

1. Walk your horse into a corner of the pen.

2. Halt.

3. Bump your horse with the calves of your legs. Start with a squeeze of both calves.

4. Repeat the squeeze.

5. Continue repeating until your horse drops his head down.

6. Immediately release any leg pressure. Pet your horse and tell him "good boy."

7. After a moment, repeat the squeezing. Even if the horse dropped his head by accident, he received the reward. He will probably drop his head sooner the second time.

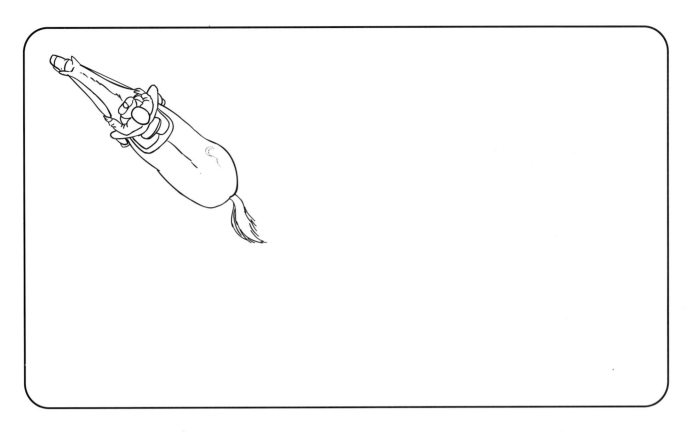

8. As soon as he drops his head, again **release pressure** and praise the horse. ▼

Connect Legs with Hands

1. Now add your rein aid. First, bump with your legs and the horse drops his head.

2. Take hold of the reins. Do not jerk with the reins. ▼

Step 8

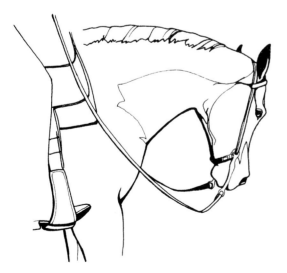

Step 2

3. Hold with the reins, bump, and the horse drops his head. Release immediately.

You're starting to make the connection between your legs and hands. The horse is now apt to give you his head. With the head in place, you can lighten up the mouth, so the horse will move without your contacting his mouth.

4. Apply rein pressure, bump your legs, and release. ▼

Step 4

5. Repeat the rein aid. The horse learns to move from the lightest feel, with his head in place.

Tips

- Persist in asking with your legs. Don't stop until your horse responds.
- Hold your horse in the corner.
- The release is the most important part of your request. When the horse gives his head, reward him. The horse experiences freedom, since you've stopped asking.
- The horse could take 10 minutes to respond. Continue asking with your legs, not with your reins.
- Don't worry about the level to which your horse drops his head. What's important is that he does respond to your aid.

Horse Sense

When you're holding your horse in the corner, don't let him move left or right or try to back up.

lesson 7

Relax the Jaw

Like the previous lesson, this exercise helps you ask a question, wait for the horse's answer, and reward the response. Colorado trainer Marge Brubaker explains how the horse must be relaxed in his jaw muscles before he can relax in the poll and body. "If you 'own' the jaw, you 'own' the horse," she says. "The resistance always starts there."

Ask your horse to respond to your cues, and give him an opportunity to answer you.

Objectives

- To encourage the horse to relax his jaw
- To learn how to communicate with the horse without pulling on the reins
- To ask the horse to give to you by using the fingertips of your little fingers on the reins

Benefits

- Your horse will not clamp his jaw and tense his body.
- Your horse will maintain forward motion.

Time Frame — Short

Step-by-Step

1. Walk your horse on a large circle to the right, at least 60 feet (20 m) in diameter.

2. Nudge him with your heel.

3. **Vibrate your inside rein, and keep a feel on the outside rein to ask the horse to give.** If you feel no response, use more leg to ask the horse to give.

   Look for the horse to open his mouth and chew the bit. Listen for him to lick his lips. Lean over and look if you can't feel it. ▼

Step 3

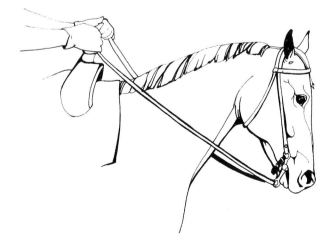

4. Immediately reward the horse as soon as he gives. Give him slack on the reins. ▶

5. Walk the entire circle on the loose rein.

6. As you begin another circle, repeat asking him to relax. Watch for him to respond more quickly the second time, and reward the relaxation.

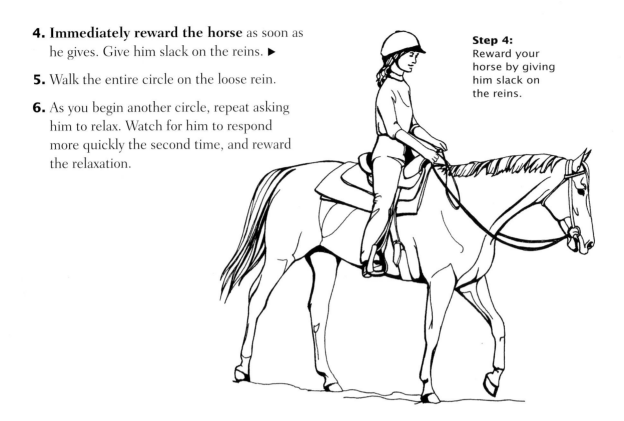

Step 4:
Reward your horse by giving him slack on the reins.

Steps 1–6

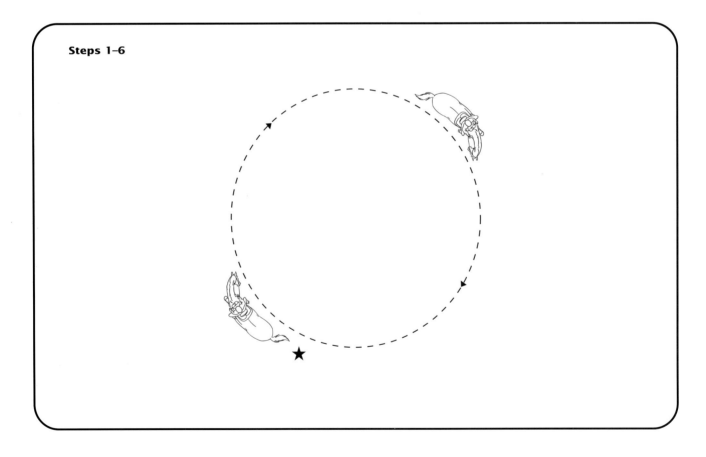

7. Walk across the circle to change direction.

8. Repeat the exercise going to the left. You may find that your horse relaxes more readily on the left side of the jaw.

9. Halt.

10. Resume the walk. Relax the jaw.

11. **Halt the horse, and lower your hands** so he will lower his head without letting it pull on you. ▼

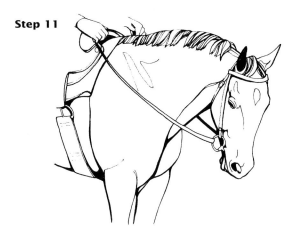

Step 11

12. Count to 5.

13. Resume the walk.

Tips

■ Ask, ask, ask, and then respond to the horse's reaction.

■ When the horse does yield, see if you can feel his back start to come up under you. Can you tell the difference between a round (rising, active) back and a hollow (dipped, stiff) back?

■ Ask less on the mouth and more on the sides to help the horse pay attention to you.

■ Be sure you release pressure when he gives his jaw.

■ Don't worry about the horse's exact head position. You want the relaxed jaw.

Horse Sense

■ Don't pull or jerk the reins.

■ Wait for the horse to answer the questions you ask.

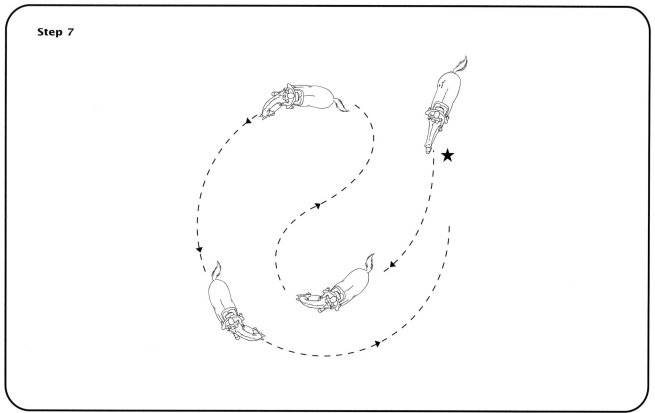

Step 7

Adjust the Brakes

You want your horse to be light and sensitive. He can feel a fly landing on his side, so he can definitely feel you shift your weight. When you lighten your cues, you ask first, and then tell. Colorado trainer Marge Brubaker follows her previous lesson with these simple patterns at the walk and the jog.

Objectives

- To lighten up the horse and sharpen his responses
- To keep your horse light through the downward and upward transitions

Benefit

Every horse should back up willingly.

Time Frame — Short

Setup

Carry a whip to school for the backup. (You will need an extension of your aids. Depending on your horse, a whip can be less irritating for him than spurs.)

Step-by-Step

At the Walk

1. Squeeze with the lower legs to walk your horse forward on a large circle.

2. Relax his jaw, as in lesson 7 on page 31.

3. When you feel his jaw is relaxed, signal for a halt. **Pick up the hands, say "whoa," and squeeze with your thighs.** Feel your horse start to stop. ▼

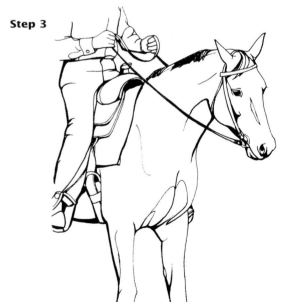

Step 3

Use your legs and reins to cue your horse for the backup. Feel him "give his chin" to you.

4. When he's stopped, count to 5.

5. Walk forward five strides.

6. Halt.

7. With a light touch, **pick up your horse with light rein contact and ask your horse to back up** four steps. You may need to cluck to the horse for the backup. ▶

8. Again squeeze with the thighs. Cluck to him as you apply leg pressure. Emphasize the signal by bumping him with your heels, or tap him once with a whip on his inside shoulder.

Keep an even pressure on both reins, unless your horse tries to back off on one side. If he does, increase the pressure on that side.

Try to keep the reins slack so you know you aren't pulling.

9. Halt. If the horse hasn't relaxed his jaw in the backup and halt, ask again for the backup. Allow him to step forward only when his head is in the right position and his jaw is relaxed.

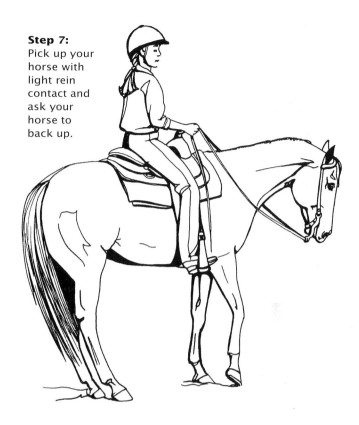

Step 7:
Pick up your horse with light rein contact and ask your horse to back up.

At the Walk

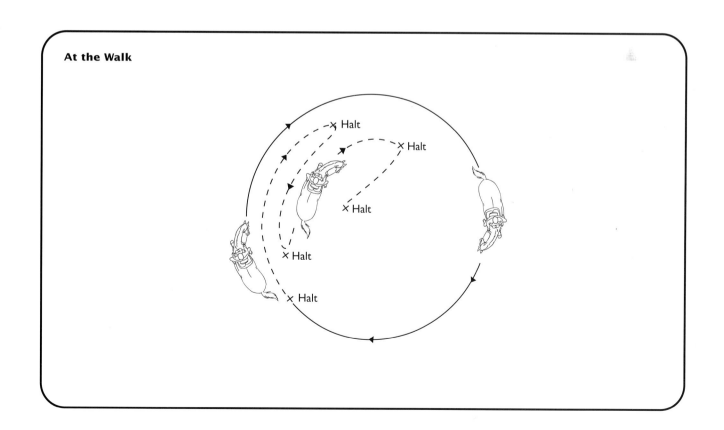

10. Cue the horse for the walk. Bring his nose in and relax the jaw.

11. Halt. This time, lower your hands when you stop. Look for the horse to lower his head and not pull.

12. Ask again for the backup. Ask lightly, to test the horse's response. Halt.

At the Jog

1. Pick up the jog on the long side.

2. Jog around the short side.

3. Halt in line with your starting point.

4. Back up.

Horse Sense

- Don't yank or jerk.
- Think ahead of the horse and act methodically.

Challenge

- Work on the horse's jaw in the trot. Keep him soft. Use a lighter rein aid to "open the door" for the horse to maintain forward motion.
- Halt. Aim for a light stop.

Tips

- If the horse raises his head and clenches his jaw when you ask for the backup, tap him with the whip. Use the whip tactfully, yet enough to impress the horse with the aid. Realize that every horse is different in his response to this cue. Err on the safe side with less of a signal, without abusing the horse.
- If the horse does not back up crisply in response to your legs, tap him with the whip on the inside shoulder. (Some riders carry two whips, one in each hand. If the horse wavers in the backup, moving crookedly, tap the whip on that side to teach him to back up straight.)
- The horse can feel your upper legs squeeze, even through the saddle.

 Focus on Form

- When you squeeze with the legs, your upper body and arms remain motionless.
- Keep your legs under you. Try standing up in the stirrups, reach forward to touch the mane, and look down at your legs. You should see only your boot toes.

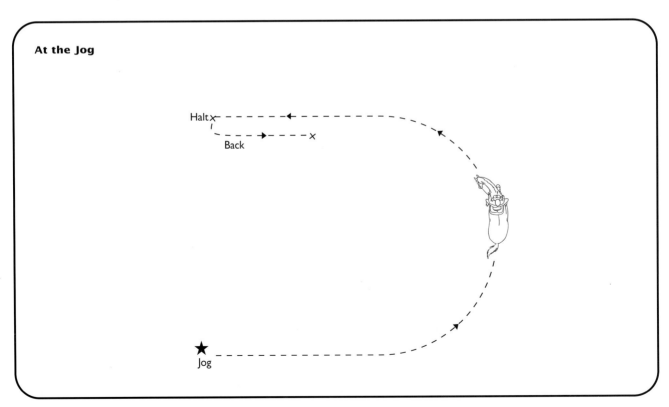

At the Jog

Halt

Back

Jog

lesson 9

Sittin' and Bittin'

A supple horse willingly reins when ridden by a skilled horseman. You can influence your horse by learning more rein "languages." New Mexico Quarter Horse trainer Carolyn Bader explains the use of two different rein cues. Practice these with two hands on the reins, and listen to how your horse replies. A "sittin' and bittin'" conversation speaks softly and with a long-lasting consequence.

Objectives

■ To learn the application and results of different reining methods

■ To pick up the reins to apply three types of rein cues

Benefits

■ These cues introduce you to lateral movements.

■ Your horse will tell you how broke he is in the mouth by the amount of cushion or softness he communicates to you.

Time Frame — Short

Recognize your horse's responses so you develop the feel of reinsmanship.

Step-by-Step

Note: Practice these rein cues while at a standstill.

Rein Cue 1: Direct Rein

1. Hold the reins in both hands, with a hand on each side of the horse's neck. Hold your hands at a height below the saddle horn.

2. **Pull back softly,** with enough tension to ask the horse to yield at the poll and loosen the jaw. At the same time, **leg the horse evenly on both sides.** Apply leg pressure to ask the horse to lower his head. When he responds, release all pressure, as shown on page 40. ▼

Rein Cue 2: Indirect Rein of Opposition

1. With your left rein, lower your hand in front of the withers.

2. Pull the indirect rein across the withers. You will displace the horse's weight to the off (right) foreleg.

3. Release.

4. With your left rein, **raise your hand behind the withers. Pull the rein toward your opposite (right) shoulder.** The horse bends, displacing his weight to the opposite (off, or right) hind leg. ▼

Rein Cue 1: Step 2

Rein Cue 2: Step 4

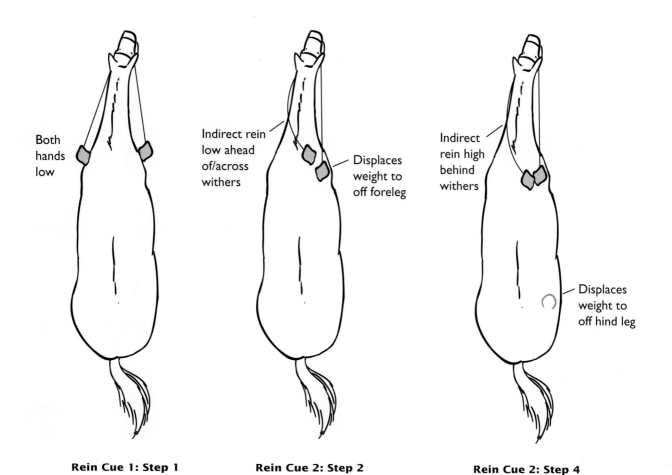

Both
hands
low

Indirect rein
low ahead
of/across
withers

Displaces
weight to
off foreleg

Indirect
rein high
behind
withers

Displaces
weight to
off hind leg

Rein Cue 1: Step 1   **Rein Cue 2: Step 2**   **Rein Cue 2: Step 4**

5. When he responds, **release all pressure.** ▶

6. Let the horse settle. Repeat with your right rein, and feel the difference.

Step 5:
Release all
pressure.

Tips

▪ Watch your wrist. This joint is often the hardest one to supple. When you pick up a rein, feel your wrist to be sure you're not stiffening this joint.

▪ Recognize what you feel. Practice this exercise before or during lessons to test the horse's response to your rein cues.

Horse Sense

▪ If you lock anywhere in your upper body — shoulder, elbow, wrist, hand, or fingers — your horse will also lock.

▪ If you stiffen anywhere in your arm from the shoulder, the horse will also stiffen against you.

Challenge

Walk your horse forward, and repeat the rein cues. Can you feel the same responses?

Idaho Isolation

Isolate the horse's forehand (front legs and shoulders) from his hindquarters (hind legs and haunches). The forefeet remain positioned, while the hind feet move step-by-step in a half-turn. The action helps you balance the horse's weight. Colorado trainer Marge Brubaker explains that learning this movement also helps you adjust signals from your rein and leg — your horse should turn, not back up or sidepass.

Objectives

▪ To turn the horse 180 degrees, moving his hindquarters around the forehand
▪ To gather your horse on his front feet so he steps over behind

Benefits

▪ The turn on the forehand will teach the horse to use his body. This exercise will help the horse improve leads at the lope and learn rollbacks and the lead change.
▪ The horse, with your foot telling him, will learn what part of his body can do what.

Time Frame — Short

Step-by-Step

1. Walk.

2. Halt so your horse stands on all four feet. Think about where you will ask your horse to go.

Your leg aid and rein cues move the horse left or right. A fence can help the horse understand that he's moving laterally, not forward.

3. To turn your horse left, **lay the right rein on his neck and drop your leg** to put the horse in position. Push the horse with your right foot. **Feel the horse anchor the front end** and walk around your calf pressure. ▼

Step 3

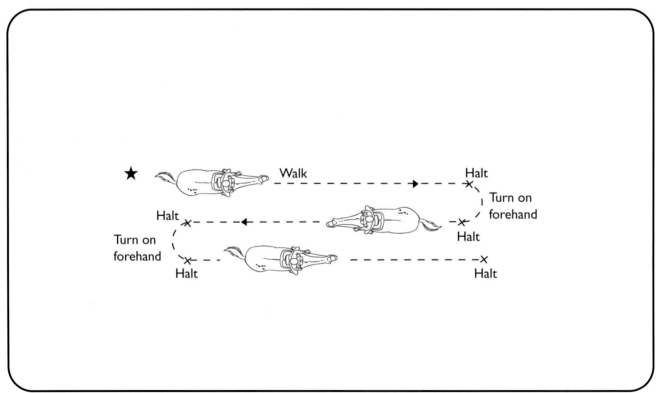

4. Continue your signals so the horse continues stepping around with the hindquarters. Keep a steady pressure with your right leg, while your rein steadies the front end.

5. When the horse faces the opposite direction from where he started, stop your signals and halt.

6. Pet him, and count to 10.

7. Walk forward ten strides.

8. Halt.

9. Ask him to turn right. **Lay the left rein on his neck, and push with the left foot.** ▼

Step 9

10. Repeat steps 5–8.

Alternate Approach

If your horse has trouble learning this movement, you can walk him into a fence corner, so his body is parallel with one fence line. Place him with the fence line on his right so he'll move left. Here you'll do a quarter-turn. With his nose in the corner, he can move only to the left. Cue him to move left. Pet him, count to ten, and then ask for the turn to the right.

Tips

- Although the horse is moving slowly, one step at a time, he should not feel "dead."
- Tighten your leg and push with your seatbone to move the horse left or right, without his losing stride or tightening up.
- Keep the horse's head and neck pointing straight forward as if you were sighting down a rifle barrel.
- Keep the horse's shoulders square.

Horse Sense

- Your horse should stand squarely before you start asking for the turn. If he's "strung out," he won't be in balance to respond properly.
- Don't tell the horse to back up or walk forward. Adjust rein pressure so he understands to move only his hindquarters to the side while his forehand remains steady.
- Avoid pulling back on the reins.
- Your horse is likely to turn more readily in one direction.

Challenge

Try the turn from a walk. Walk forward, check the horse with a slight vibration of the reins, and ask for the turn.

 Focus on Form

- Watch your leg position and heels when you signal for the turn.
- Remember, left rein and left leg to go right; right rein and right leg to go left.

Break Up the Drive Train

California reining horse trainer Gary Ferguson builds on the concept of yielding to pressure. His horses learn how to give at the hip, rib cage, and shoulders. Gary calls these "breaking points." With your rein and leg, you control these body parts. Being able to pick up a shoulder or move a hip helps you improve transitions, preventing the horse from "locking up" or resisting your aids.

Objectives

- To control the placement of the horse's body
- To move the horse's hips, rib cage, or shoulders right or left
- To control parts of the horse's body separately

Rein and leg cue the horse to yield.

Benefits

- You will improve control of the entire horse by controlling the parts.
- You will soften the horse's responses to your cues. The horse becomes soft on the inside as he yields to pressure.
- You can put the horse where you want him. When you can place any part of the horse, you'll be prepared for movements like the flying change of lead.
- You will improve your independent seat, moving your hands, legs, and weight separately.

Time Frame — Short

Step-by-Step

1. Walk the horse forward. Your legs should drape around the barrel.

2. First move the hip over. **Move your left leg back 3 or 4 inches (8–10 cm). Squeeze your calf** to feel the horse give to the pressure. The horse should shift his hip to the right. ▼

3. Release pressure. Walk forward two strides and halt.

4. Next move the rib cage over. Your left leg should be in a straight, hanging position. **Squeeze at the cinch with your left leg.** You want to feel the bend. ▼

Step 4

Step 2

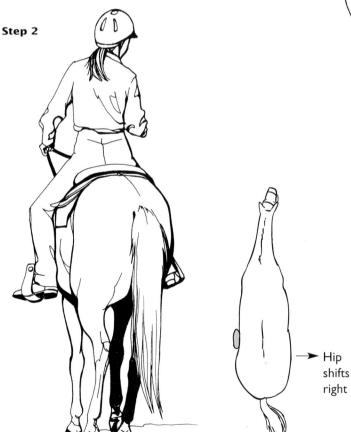

Hip shifts right

5. Release pressure. Walk forward two strides and halt.

6. Now **move the shoulders over with your outside** (in this case, left) **rein.** Feel that you "pick up" the shoulders to the right. ▼

Step 6

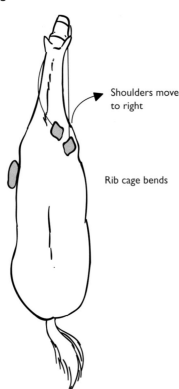

Shoulders move to right

Rib cage bends

7. Release pressure. Walk your horse in a large circle, on a loose rein.

8. Halt, and reverse the signals so you **move the horse to the left,** one part at a time. ▼

Step 8

Tips

■ Always think about moving the horse from back to front.

■ Feel how your legs control the hip and rib cage, while your rein controls the shoulder and poll.

■ With repetition, the horse should start to move his hip as soon as your leg moves back.

■ Some trainers talk about "opening doors" on the horse. Your rein and leg cues each open or close a door, or one of the four quadrants around each leg. This results in control of the horse's body.

Horse Sense

Understand that the horse's back doesn't bend. The horse bends from the shoulders forward; you can "rock" the rib cage to supple it.

lesson 12

Circle Up

Look between your horse's ears and envision a circle ahead of you. Now guide him along the shape, stride by stride. Even walking, this simple pattern demands that you prepare your horse for bending and turning.

The imaginary line that you follow helps you improve your eye and ride where you look. Maintain rhythm and balance, stay soft and relaxed, and plan your moves for smooth arcs.

Objectives
- To bend the horse correctly on a circle
- To use your hands and legs to arc the horse on circles of various sizes
- To use the turn on the forehand to help your horse keep his shoulders up

Benefits
- You will develop your eye for a continuously curved line.
- You will understand how your horse can flex on a circle.
- The horse will circle in balance, without ducking in and cutting the circle.

Time Frame — Medium

Setup
Set up two cones, about 30 feet (10 m) apart on a straight line, away from a fence.

Step-by-Step
1. Walk to Cone 1.

2. At Cone 1, start applying aids to arc the horse to the left, toward Cone 2. Drop your inside (left) hip and lightly squeeze your left leg. Feel the left rein. Look to see the corner of the horse's left eye, as he drops his head and turns.

You and your horse circle together, with you guiding him along the shape you visualize.

3. Walk around Cone 2. Take a mental snapshot: Did you stay on the arc from Cone 1 to Cone 2, in the circle's first half? ▼

Step 3

4. Continue walking the second half of the circle, toward Cone 1.

5. Walk to the outside of Cone 1, and halt when your boot heel is aligned with the cone.

6. Turn the horse a half-turn on the forehand to face right. Halt. Cone 1 should be ahead of your horse.

7. Walk the same size circle to the right. Take more mental snapshots of your position, midway between each cone.

8. Repeat the half-turn when you again arrive at Cone 1.

9. Halt. Dismount, and move Cone 1 approximately 10 feet (3 m) closer to Cone 2.

10. Repeat both circles and turns on the forehand.

ARENA SEQUENCE

Steps 1–5

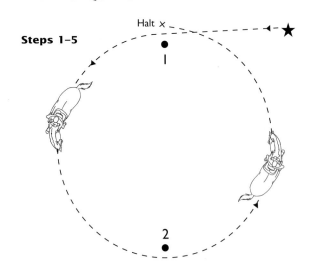

Steps 6 and 7

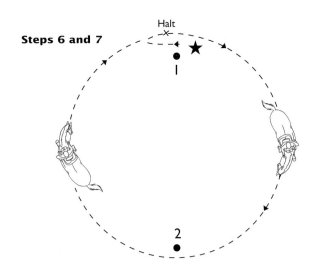

Tips

- Is each circle round? Horses tend to wander, and you might end up forming an oval, rectangle, or other polygon. Can you pinpoint where your horse started to deviate?
- Did your horse listen to your signals?
- Did your horse really bend? Look for him to bend from the shoulders, with "give" in the rib cage.
- You should see that his inside ear is back, to signal that he is bending. His pace should not change.

Horse Sense

As you bend the horse, watch that he doesn't cant his head to the outside by lifting his nose in resistance.

Challenge

- Practice the pattern without stirrups. Can you maintain your balance?
- Trot the pattern.
- Lope the pattern.
- For tighter walk circles, move the cones even closer together.

Focus on Form

- Keep your chin level as you look for the bend.
- Your inside leg asks for the bend.
- Even as you bend, ask your horse to maintain rhythm. Squeeze with the outside leg to move him up if he slows.

Step 8

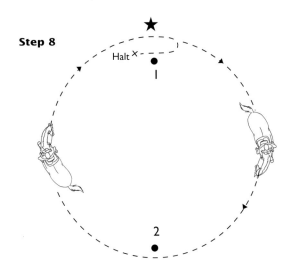

Step 10

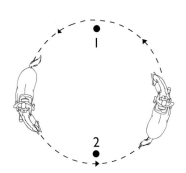

Serpentine Circus

Transitions through the three gaits challenge your eyes and sense of rhythm. You want to feel your horse bend through serpentines at a consistent speed, with the softened jaw you practiced in this chapter's earlier lessons. Every time you turn at a cone, ask yourself if your horse feels level and relaxed. On the loops, prevent his drifting out or cutting in. And watch that your legs remain steady so you sit still on the pattern.

Objectives

- To help the horse relax through the serpentine exercise
- To guide your horse through serpentine loops at all three gaits, forming loops of the same size, shape, and placement
- To improve your eye as you plan your transitions

Benefits

- Turning on the loops of the serpentine will help your horse become supple.
- The serpentine will help relax a hot, fresh horse.
- Turning will help you and your horse think and listen.

Time Frame — Medium

Setup

An area with at least 130 feet (40 m) in each direction. Arrange four cones, as shown opposite.

Step-by-Step

Crosswise Loops

1. Walking left from Cone 4, aim to the right of Cone 1.

Look for a feeling of softness on straight lines and on the loops of a series of turns.

2. Walk around Cone 1, making a wide loop.

3. Make a second wide loop, starting your arc right to line up between Cones 4 and 3, and then turn right again to aim to the right of Cone 2.

4. Walk around Cone 2, making a wide loop. The loop should be the same size and shape as the one you made around Cone 1.

5. Aim to the left of Cone 3. **Walk around Cone 3,** making a wide loop. The loop should be the same size and shape as the one you made between Cones 4 and 3. ▶

6. Walk a straight line, parallel to the line you made walking to Cone 3, to complete this loop.

7. Turn right when you're lined up with Cone 2.

8. Walk past Cone 2, with it to your right, aiming to the left of Cone 1.

9. Walk a circle to the right, 30 feet (10 m) in diameter, around Cone 1.

10. Halt, and pet your horse.

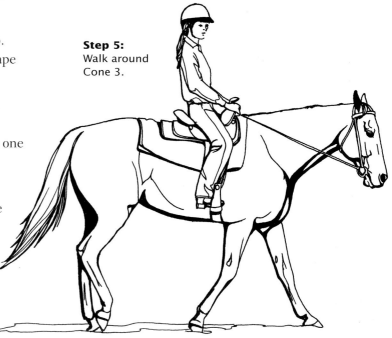

Step 5:
Walk around Cone 3.

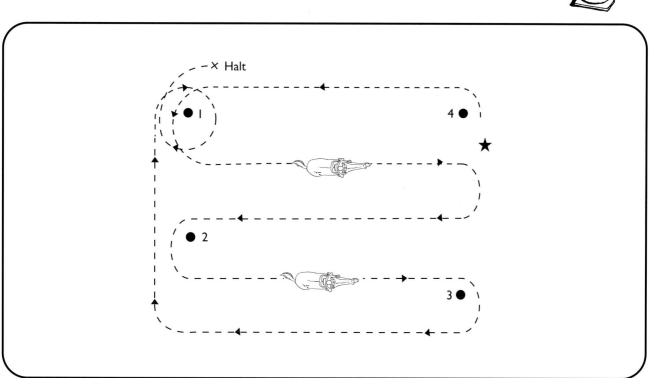

Tightened Loops

1. Resume walking toward the left of Cone 4.

2. Two strides before Cone 4, **pick up the jog.** ▼

Step 2

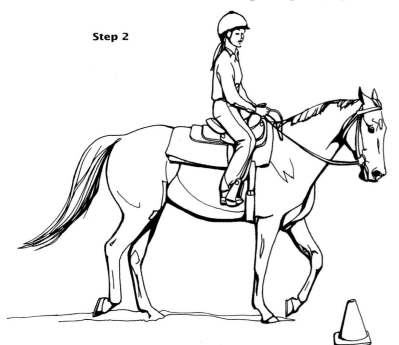

3. Turn right around Cone 4, in a smaller loop, about 20 feet (6 m) in diameter. Keep your horse jogging at the same speed in the loop; do not let him slow down or speed up.

4. Jog half the length of the distance between Cones 1 and 4.

5. Turn left, again in a 20-foot (6 m) loop. Jog toward point between Cones 3 and 4.

6. Turn right, in the third 20-foot (6 m) loop.

7. Jog toward the right of Cone 2, making a wide loop, about 30 feet (10 m), around Cone 2.

8. Jog toward the left of Cone 3, making a wide loop around Cone 3.

9. Slow to the walk, turn the corner, and walk to the left of Cone 1.

10. Halt at Cone 1.

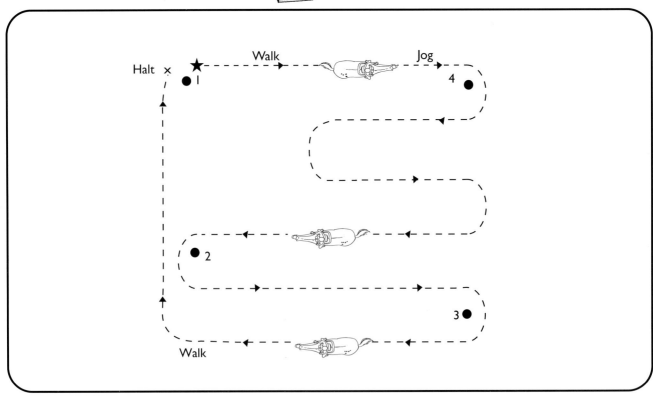

Lengthwise Loops

1. From the halt, do a half-turn on the forehand.

2. To start the lengthwise loops, pick up the jog toward Cone 2.

3. Pass Cone 2 on the right.

4. Thirty feet (10 m) beyond Cone 2, turn left. Make a wide loop, and jog toward the right of Cone 1.

5. Turn right when you're lined up with Cone 1. Make a wide loop.

6. Jog down to make a wide loop, lined up with the first one you made in this direction.

7. You will now make two shorter serpentine loops, each half the size of the first loops in this direction. Turn right, using Cones 4 and 3 as markers.

8. Aiming toward the right of Cone 3, jog down to make the last loop around Cone 3.

9. Halt past Cone 3.

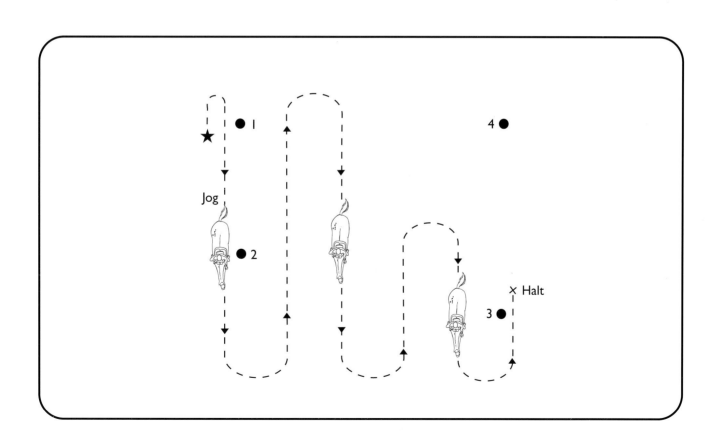

Loping the Loops

1. Walk your horse on a half-circle, to end up to the right of Cone 3, facing in the direction of Cone 2.

2. Pick up the lope on the right lead, aiming to the left of Cone 2.

3. Make a wide loop around Cone 2.

4. Do a simple change of lead halfway before the second loop. Drop to a trot for two strides, then **pick up the left lead.** ▶

5. Make a wide loop, between Cones 3 and 4.

6. Do a simple change of lead halfway before the third loop.

7. Make a wide loop, between Cones 2 and 1.

Step 4:
Pick up the left lead.

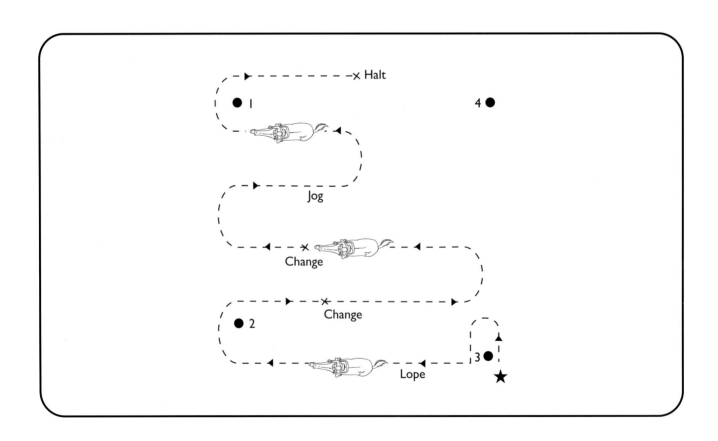

8. Slow to the jog, and make a smaller loop to the left. Use Cones 1 and 4 as markers. ▶

9. Aim to the left of Cone 1. Jog around Cone 1.

10. Halt halfway between Cones 1 and 4. Pet your horse.

Tips

- Keep using your signals on the loops.
- Be aware of your horse's attitude.
- Listen for signs of resistance on the loops. Where did your horse resist? Did he circle evenly to left and right? Were his arcs consistent?

Horse Sense

- Watch that the horse stays consistent in his strides, whether he's going forward or turning.
- Avoid allowing the horse to fall on the forehand as you change the diameter of the loops. Use your leg to urge the horse forward.

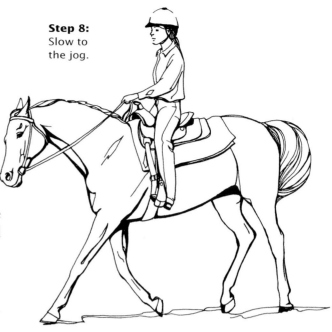

Step 8: Slow to the jog.

Chapter 3 Summary

Lessons in this chapter helped you practice movements that supple and relax your horse. You're beginning to realize the challenges of horsemanship. Riding well isn't easy. To guide the horse when he wants to resist demands courage, determination, and persistence.

Don't give up if your horse doesn't want to do what you ask. Continue asking him to cooperate with you. To encourage him toward relaxation and suppleness, remain calm and relaxed yourself. Your horse will reflect your emotional state. Remember to breathe, and keep your face calm. If you clench your jaw, your horse is likely to tense his.

- Do you look and think ahead?
- Are you starting to ask more, and look for the response?
- How does your horse move away from your leg?
- How does he try to escape your signals? Does he consistently attempt the same evasions, under the same circumstances?
- Does your horse try to pull you out of balance?

- Do you feel you have a consistent seat? Do you keep a straight line, from the back of your head down through your shoulder and hip to your heel?
- Can you move hands and legs independently?
- Do you think "lightness" when you signal your horse?
- Do you use your leg when necessary — not all the time to make your horse "dead to the leg," yet always when you need to cue the horse?
- Does your upper body stay upright?
- Your seat helps your horse to perform. If your seat isn't steady, remember to check your position frequently. Adjust your position, and think about sitting quietly and in the middle of the horse. You must remain in balance with your horse before you ask more of him in subsequent lessons.
- A supple horse is listening to you. He is a better broke horse. You'll build on his responses in the lessons in chapter 4. These will give you more opportunities to improve communication and your horse's flexibility, so your horse is "on the aids." You'll also start working more on the quality of your horse's gaits.

At any gait, your equine partner awaits your next signal of leg, seat, or rein.

chapter 4

Readiness

Your Western horse doesn't perform on contact, yet he accepts the bit. The ideal performer works on a loose rein and is still "on the aids." He is relaxed yet alert. He listens for your signal and responds immediately to your cue, no matter how subtle.

To train the horse to this level, you signal him with legs, weight, and hands. You communicate as lightly as possible, always moving toward lighter commands. You'll want to feel a constant response from your horse so he feels as if he's "on the bit" even when reins are slack. When you do apply rein contact, you are not abrupt or hurried and neither is your horse.

This chapter builds on earlier lessons. Your horse should feel rhythmic and relaxed, and now you'll ask for more. As you increase your requests, be ready for an exuberant reaction. Don't get after a horse when he gives you more than you asked for — you want him to try hard to please you.

Your horse may answer you reluctantly and increase his resistance. Remember that horses can be devious, and few are truly honest. Anticipate how your horse will react, give him the chance to respond, and cue accordingly. Leave him alone when he's good, and signal him when he needs guidance.

Approach these lessons riding a horse that exhibits suppleness started in the jaw. A relaxed jaw leads a supple body and ultimately the clever footwork of the finished horse. If your horse becomes tense, you can backtrack to repeat earlier lessons.

You'll look for more accuracy and a quicker response in these patterns. You'll ask for smooth transitions, such as a change of pace upward (walk to the jog, jog to the long trot, trot to the lope) and downward (lope to the trot, trot to the jog, jog to the walk). Your aim is upward transitions that are willingly forward and downward shifts that are obediently slow.

Patterns based on the circle will ask your horse to balance himself. As you perform full circles, half-circles, and arcs, you'll discover that such simple shapes are difficult, if not impossible, to duplicate with your horse's tracks. To form these shapes, you'll need to develop your eye so your horse goes where you look. Always visualize the figure before you start. You might "play a movie" in your mind so you know where you'll go when you cue your horse.

To check your horse's balance, you'll test how he carries his head, neck, back, and croup. Instead of your "holding" him, you want to feel that he's maintaining himself in balance, with minimal signals from you. From the saddle, you should see and feel that he's dropping from the withers. He shouldn't be "strung out," or unbalanced from back to front. Look for the feeling of softness on the inside as you bend.

These lessons introduce riding one-handed. The Western horse traditionally works from the neck rein. You hold the reins in one hand, carried slightly above the saddle horn. To signal right or left, you lay a rein on the horse's neck.

Fingertip Controls

The broke horse is light in the mouth. Whatever bit he carries, he listens to and acknowledges the slightest signal. Even though the finished Western horse performs "off" the bit, you still have some rein contact as you signal your horse. You want to feel him accept the bit, so you cultivate a good mouth by giving and taking rein contact. Learn your horse's responses and evaluate your reinsmanship through these two "hands-on" tests.

Objectives

▪ To feel how lightly you can handle the reins to signal your horse

Your fingers feel the horse's mouth as you give and take the rein contact.

▪ To prepare your horse for a consistent response
▪ To lengthen or shorten the reins smoothly
▪ To improve how you give and take through your hands
▪ To become aware of the slightest movement of your hands
▪ To adjust the rein so you put the horse in balance from the face

Benefits

▪ The horse will feel every move you make on the reins. Subtle rein adjustment shouldn't upset the horse or make him anticipate.
▪ The broke horse will be light and responsive to a quiet rein hand.
▪ You'll ride more humanely.
▪ Your horse will maintain a natural headset.

Time Frame — Short

Setup

A pen. Arrange a single cone in the middle. Use colored "rainbow" reins, with different colored sections. Or, you can wrap colored or electrical tape around reins at 6-inch (15 cm) intervals.

Step-by-Step

Testing at the Walk

1. Walk your horse in a straight line toward the cone on a loose rein. Get a picture in your mind of how you expect your horse to carry himself.

How does he carry his neck and head? See how his neck comes out of his chest, and look at his spine as he travels. "Take a snapshot" in your mind of what you want to feel in the saddle.

2. Look straight ahead, through your horse's ears. Feel both hands contacting the horse's mouth. Sense which rein is where in each hand. Shorten the reins by walking your fingers down the reins, or by sliding your hands. ▼

Step 2

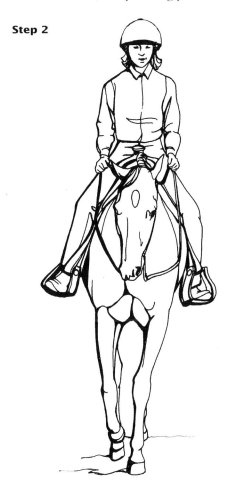

3. Stop shortening the reins when you feel the first touch of contact with your horse's mouth. How does your horse respond when you feel the bit in his mouth? ▼

Step 3

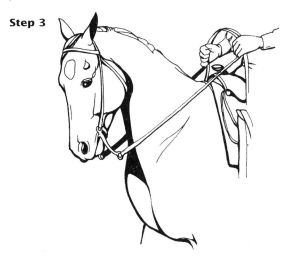

4. See if you can ask your horse to relax his jaw with your little fingers.

5. Lengthen the reins again so they drape by the horse's shoulder. ▼

Step 5

Focus on Form

- Have your assistant make a videotape of you practicing this exercise. Determine whether what you see on the tape is what you feel in the saddle.
- Hold the reins efficiently.

6. Shorten the reins so they're loose, yet just before you feel contact.

7. Move your right rein to the side, without any contact. Know when to pause after you lengthen or shorten, so you don't cue the horse.

From what you've practiced, decide what is the appropriate length of rein. You should be able to move your hand forward and back to feel and release contact.

8. Close your hands to apply pressure to halt. ▼

Step 8

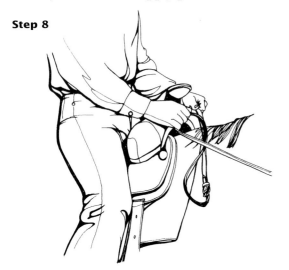

9. Adjust your hand movement to respond to the horse. Lift and let go. Follow the take with a give. Glance at the poll. Do you feel the horse extend his neck when you give? Push him with the alternate leg.

Testing at the Jog

1. Pick up the jog, and feel your hands. Do they bounce or float steadily? Close your leg and feel if your horse is soft. Does he feel ready to yield when you ask for a transition?

2. Slow to the walk, and form a large circle with the cone in the middle.

3. While turning on the circle, **use your outside rein to keep the horse from dropping his shoulder.** This rein reminds the horse to stay flexed and bent. ▶

4. Change direction, and pick up the jog. Use legs and reins, in coordination, to change direction at the cone.

Tips

▪ Feel the horse move freely with his head and shoulders.
▪ The horse is not on the bit when he pulls at every stride.

Horse Sense

▪ Don't cramp up the horse's natural position. The horse can feel alive, but he shouldn't come behind the bit.
▪ The horse might take advantage of you as you adjust your reins. He could push forward with his face or raise his head too high.
▪ Your horse may overflex if you use your hands too strongly.
▪ Avoid these rein handling mistakes: raising your hand to make contact, handling reins like a handful of thorns, or using an obvious "milking" motion.

Challenge

▪ Try to adjust the reins invisibly. Have an assistant make a video that focuses on your hands. Are you obvious in your hand movements?
▪ Practice with one hand.

Step 3:
Use your outside rein to keep the horse from dropping his shoulder.

Striding and Guiding

New Mexico trainer Carolyn Bader led you through "Sittin' and Bittin'" in chapter 3. Now you'll apply direct and indirect rein cues to guide your horse in arcs. The curve of the horse's body will match the curve of the exercise. You'll start with coordinating two hands on the reins and flex your horse on the circle. Test your progress by guiding with your outside rein.

Objectives

- To direct the horse's line of motion with your inside and outside hands
- To guide the horse's stride on a round circle
- To move the horse's shoulder over with the reins

Benefits

- Combining the direct and indirect rein aids will help you guide the horse on a circle.
- Bending at the walk and trot will teach the horse to circle correctly. You'll be ready to guide the horse at the lope, where he's more likely to lean into the circle.

Time Frame — Short

Setup

A pen. Arrange a single cone anywhere in the pen, well away from a fence or a wall.

The outside rein signals the horse to arc his body.

Step-by-Step

1. Walk your horse to 20 feet (6 m) from the cone, and circle left. Maintain a circle of an equal distance, using the cone as your center.

2. Ask for an inside arc. **Pull the inside (left) rein softly so you create the arc. Apply slight pressure with your inside leg.** Your right (outside) rein controls the shoulder from "leaking out" on the circle, or losing the arc. Keep your outside leg off the horse unless it's needed to push him forward, or he drifts to the outside with his haunch. You should see the horse's left nostril and eye. ▶

3. Walk twice around the cone to the left.

4. Halt. Ask yourself if your circles were both exactly round. Was the cone always 20 feet (6 m) from your left foot?

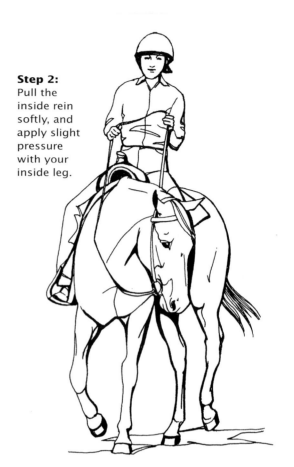

Step 2: Pull the inside rein softly, and apply slight pressure with your inside leg.

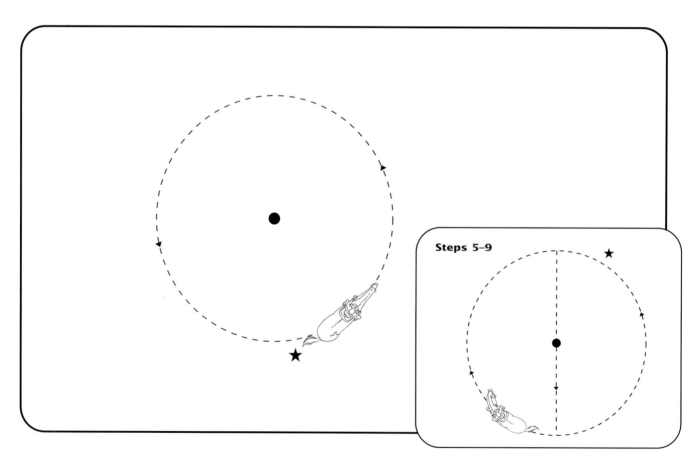

Steps 5–9

5. Turn and walk across the circle so you can walk in the opposite direction. Be sure that you use both reins. You want to feel that the horse expects to feel the outside rein and will bend away from this indirect rein. Aim for a light touch of the rein.

6. Halt and check your progress traveling to the right.

7. Pick up the jog, and jog the circle twice to the right. ▼

Step 7

8. Halt and check your progress.

9. Turn, and jog the circle twice to the left.

Tips

- Think of your circle as a series of straight lines, redirected into this figure.
- Visualize your rein signals as "opening doors" to the horse.
- You want to make the horse very conscious of the outside rein. Never take hold of the inside rein unless the horse first feels the outside rein against the neck. The outside rein tells him where to follow his head so you can lighten the use of your inside rein.

Horse Sense

- Understand the control you should use with your outside rein and hand. If you pull with just the inside rein, you're likely to unbalance the horse. He may start rubbernecking (bending only with his neck) rather than giving with the shoulder, or pushing the shoulder out too far, off the track. When he's unbalanced, he can't use his loin and haunches as well.
- Sometimes the faster movement of the jog straightens and relaxes the horse, making it easier for you to bend on the circle. However, speed can increase the horse's tendency to lean in rather than arc. The horse can try to find the shortest way around the circle.

Challenge

- Work in the one-handed riding as you advance.
- Try this at the lope, increasing the distance to 30 feet (10 m) from the cone.

Stay on Track

Building on the previous lesson, you'll expand your guiding skills to the reverse arc. The flexions you request help your horse concentrate on your hands and legs. Ask for the response, and learn to recognize the changes in the horse's body between an arc and a reverse arc. This lesson tests your horse's willingness to allow you to dictate to him.

Objectives

- To follow a bent line, maintaining the arc to inside or outside
- To guide the horse using direct and indirect rein on the circle

Flex your horse to the inside of the bend, shifting his hindquarters with your leg aid.

- To use your reins and legs independently to help the horse circle with his shoulders up
- To bend your horse in an arc, and then a reverse arc

Benefits

- Your hands will work together, along with your legs.
- Switching from arc to reverse arc will encourage your horse to "listen" to your legs.

Time Frame — Short

Setup

Arrange three cones, 15 feet (4.5 m) apart.

Step-by-Step

Before you start this pattern, think about the controls you practiced in lessons 5 (page 22) and 7 (page 31).

Arc

1. At Cone 1, start to walk the first half of a circle to the left, toward Cone 3.

2. **Arc the horse left by pressing your inside (left) leg on the cinch. Hold your inside (left) rein slightly to the side,** and feel the horse "seek" support of the outside (right) rein. ▶

3. **Hold the outside rein against the horse's neck, as the indirect rein aid. Nudge with your inside leg** to remind the horse to bend and to push the shoulder to the outside. Push him with the alternate leg so he moves forward as he steps over in the arc. Feel the outside thrust in the arc.

    If the horse starts to "bulge" the shoulder too far out, press your outside (right) leg behind the cinch. You should feel as if you are containing the horse within both hands and legs. ▶

4. At Cone 3, allow the horse to walk on a straight line for four strides.

5. Halt.

Arc

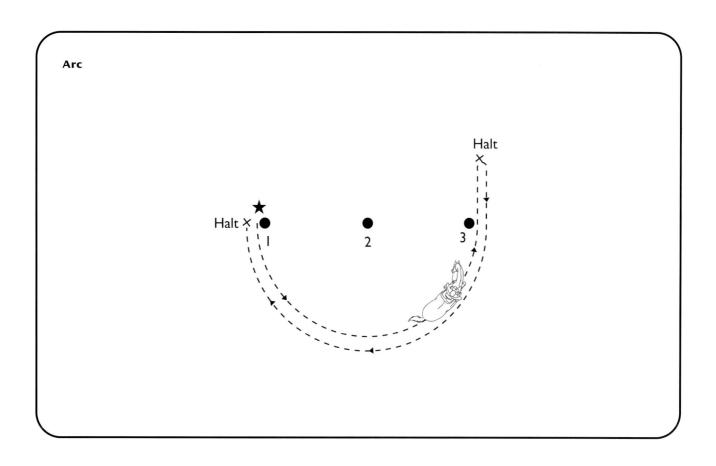

Step 2:
Arc the horse left by pressing inside leg on cinch; hold inside rein slightly to the side.

Step 3:
Hold the outside rein against the horse's neck; nudge with your inside leg.

6. Turn on the forehand, and walk a straight line back to Cone 3.

7. At Cone 3, **start to walk another first half of a circle to the right.** ▼

Step 7

8. Repeat Steps 2 and 3, arcing the horse right.

9. At Cone 1, halt and pet your horse.

Reverse Arc

1. Resume the walk on the circle to the right.

2. Two steps into the circle right, ask the horse to move the shoulder left while circling right. Your reins move the shoulder over, as you open the outside (left) rein and push with the inside (right). Use the inside (right) leg to push the shoulders out.

   The horse's head remains to the inside. You should feel the forehand "sweep." Keep the shoulders up and to the outside.

3. When you feel the shoulder move out and stay in the reverse arc, ask again for a straight line. Move the shoulder back in.

4. Halt.

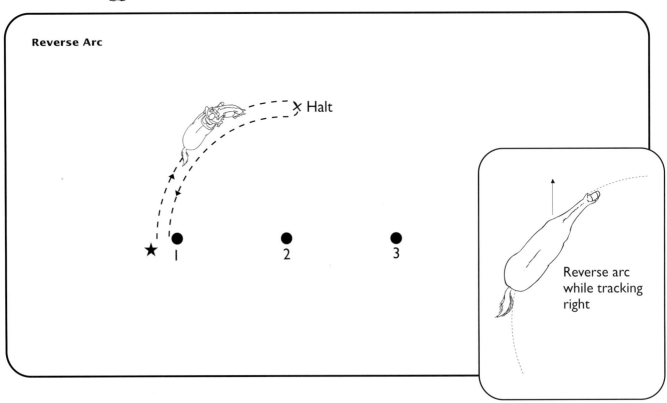

Reverse Arc

✗ Halt

★ ● ● ●
   1 2 3

Reverse arc while tracking right

5. Do a half-turn on the forehand so you face left, toward Cone 1.

6. Resume the walk.

7. Try the reverse arc to the left. You will move the shoulder right while circling left, so reverse your aids. **Push with the inside rein, open the outside rein, and use your inside leg.** ▼

Step 7

8. Ask again for the straight line.

9. Halt at Cone 1, and pet your horse.

Focus on Form

Sit deep. Remember that you'll be using both hands and legs, while maintaining a straight, even position.

Tips

■ Experiment with how much aid to apply to keep your horse on the arc. Bend the horse's body, not just his neck. If you see his neck bend but feel that his body is straight and stiff, he's in a "rubberneck" position.

■ The body follows the shoulder and nose.

■ If the horse isn't using the shoulders, correct with your rein. If he isn't using his hip, correct with your leg.

■ In the reverse arc, you push, not pull.

Horse Sense

■ Don't hold the inside rein too close to the withers.

■ Watch that you don't restrict the horse with your aids. Allow him to maintain his rhythm.

■ The horse will probably wander off the track. Keep alert, and adjust your aids.

Challenge

Try the arc and reverse arc at the jog.

Mirrored Hackamore

You'll probably ride this pattern with a bridle and bit, but you'll form the shape of a bosal as a half-circle. The pattern tests your horse's right and left bending. It also tests how well you use your eyes to plan your pattern, and how you can plan ahead to replicate the shape. Think about when and how much to use your leg and rein, and when to quit sending a signal.

Objectives
- To guide the horse in half-circle patterns, keeping him listening and reacting to your signals
- To form a half-circle in reverse, then copy the same number of steps and shape to the opposite side

To bend, know when to start, maintain, and quit using your leg and rein aids.

- To ride a smooth figure, where your horse comes around readily to your cues

Benefits
- Your horse will listen more intently to the leg pressure you practiced in chapter 2.
- You'll keep your horse in balance, not strung out (dragging behind and not reaching forward with the hind legs).
- You will develop your eye.
- If you show, you'll reverse using the half-circle (usually away from the rail in the show pen).

Time Frame — Medium

Setup
The fence line of an arena, or a wall. Place a single cone along the boundary, as shown opposite.

Step-by-Step
1. Walk along the rail, toward the cone, with the horse's left shoulder to the outside.

2. At the cone, walk your horse out from the rail for four strides. **Cue first with your leg,** then with the outside rein. ▼

Step 2

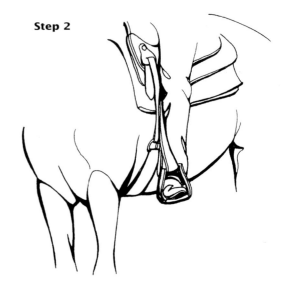

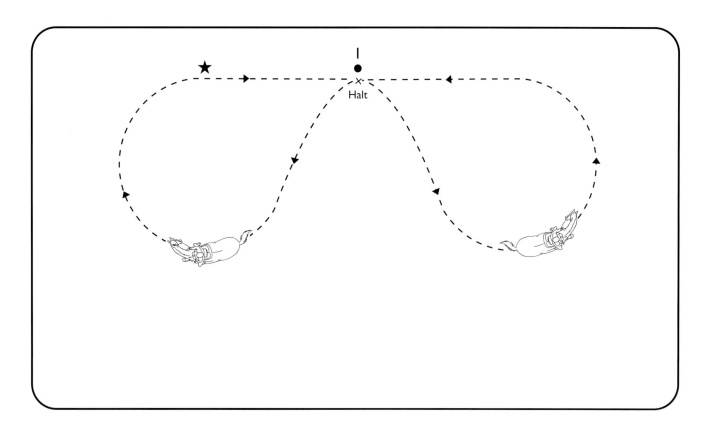

Halt

3. On the fifth stride, apply aids to begin the half-circle back toward the rail, so you form the shape of a hackamore. **Apply your inside leg for the bend, and feel your horse seek the support of the outside rein.** Continue to count the strides it takes to arrive back at the rail. ▼

Step 3

4. You complete the half-circle back at the rail. Continue walking in a straight line, still counting strides, and halt at the cone.

5. Repeat the half-circle going in the other direction. Aim to match the same number of strides that you used to form the first hackamore shape.

   How does the horse respond to your inside leg, outside rein? Do you need to use the inside rein and outside leg to maintain the half-circle?

6. Halt at the cone, and pet your horse. Ask yourself whether you formed two identical shapes. Did your horse feel balanced or strung out? Did he change his rhythm or fall on the forehand? Which shape was better — to the right or to the left?

7. Repeat the figure. Try to improve the shapes by correcting your horse's evasions.

8. Reverse the figure. Walk on the rail, and turn away from the rail to form your half-circles.

Tips
- Have a plan before you start. Keep a strong, elastic form as you guide through the shapes.
- Look for the horse to turn without hesitation.
- After your first try, let your horse relax at the walk.
- Keep your horse "alive" in this figure. If he starts to slow or speed up, adjust his pace.

Horse Sense
- Don't be quick, or rush.
- Watch that your horse stays on the track and doesn't drift toward his stronger side.

Challenge
- Walk the first hackamore, and trot the second. Keep a steady rhythm, not fast or "dead."
- Trot to form a larger figure, by adding three more strides.
- Trot to form a smaller figure, by subtracting three strides.
- Practice the figure away from the rail.
- Practice without stirrups to test your balance.

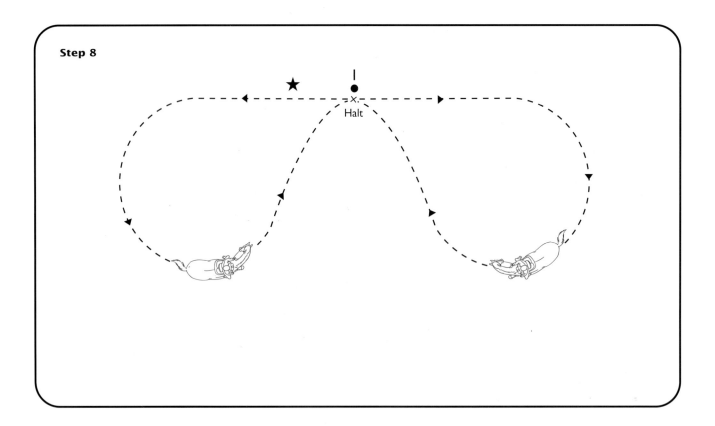

Step 8

Halt

lesson 18

Sidepassing

Like the other lessons in this chapter, this exercise differs from typical "rail work." You ask for a controlled maneuver, one step at a time. The sidepass tests your feel, timing, and balance for a refined movement. It shows your control of the horse laterally, from side to side, rather than longitudinally, or from back to front. A useful exercise to intersperse in faster work, sidepassing asks the horse to stop and listen.

Objectives

- To teach the horse to move from your leg, without going forward or back
- To cue your horse to step readily to either side

Benefits

- Sidepassing will make your horse more flexible.
- In shows or when trail riding, you will be able to move your horse to the side in a lineup or maneuver through an obstacle.

To start the sidepass, you keep the horse "in front" of your legs to signal.

Time Frame — Short

Setup

Before sidepassing, warm up with other exercises on a straight line or circles. A fence or a wall will be needed as a barrier to prevent the horse from moving forward.

Step-by-Step

1. Walk your horse toward the wall or fence, and halt when his nose is no closer than 2 feet (0.5 m) to the barrier.

2. Cue your horse to move to the left. Move your right (outside) leg forward, while your reins keep the horse straight. Lay the right rein on the horse's neck, move your left hand out to the side, and press with the right leg. Your left leg remains still. You should see your horse tip his head slightly to the left.

3. Sidepass a full step to the left. Halt. You may have to drive with your right hip, pushing your weight in the direction you want to move. ▼

Step 3

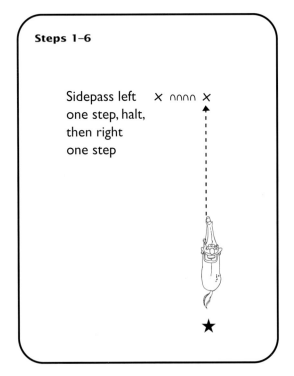

Sidepass left one step, halt, then right one step

Steps 1–6

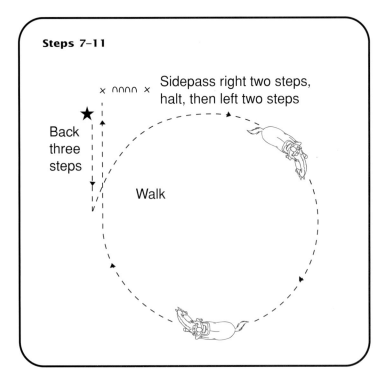

Steps 7–11

Sidepass right two steps, halt, then left two steps

Back three steps

Walk

4. Pet the horse, and count to 10.

5. Ask the horse to move to the right. **Reverse your signals,** pressing with the left leg and using the left neck rein. Hold the right rein out to the side. ▼

Step 5

6. Halt and pet. Is your horse more willing to move to the left or the right?

7. Back up three steps.

8. Walk forward on a large circle, on a loose rein.

9. Halt back at the fence or wall.

10. Sidepass right two steps, then halt. ▼

Step 10

11. Sidepass left two steps, then halt.

Tip

You might choose to carry a whip while first practicing this lesson. Tap the horse on the shoulder or hindquarters to teach him to move over.

Horse Sense

▪ The horse may start to turn on the hindquarter. Nudge with your leg and close your left hand.

▪ The horse may turn so he's crooked. Correct him, without holding him back with the reins.

Nevada Neck Rein

Not just in Nevada — the neck rein is basic training for every Western horse. You lay the rein against the neck, and he turns. Release the rein, and he resumes the straight line. Colorado trainer Marge Brubaker's exercise isn't for a green horse; it tests the reinability of the trained horse. You'll coordinate your use of the reins, as you start with two hands and then switch to one.

Objectives

▪ To teach the horse to turn at the weight of the rein on his neck
▪ To guide your horse right and left, using the neck rein

Benefit

The neck rein is basic to Western riding. If you plan to show, you will be expected to ride one-handed in horsemanship, equitation, pleasure, trail, and reining classes.

Time Frame — Medium

Setup

Arrange five cones, set 15 feet (4.5 m) apart, as shown opposite.

The horse waits for you to place the rein on his neck, signaling him to turn left or right.

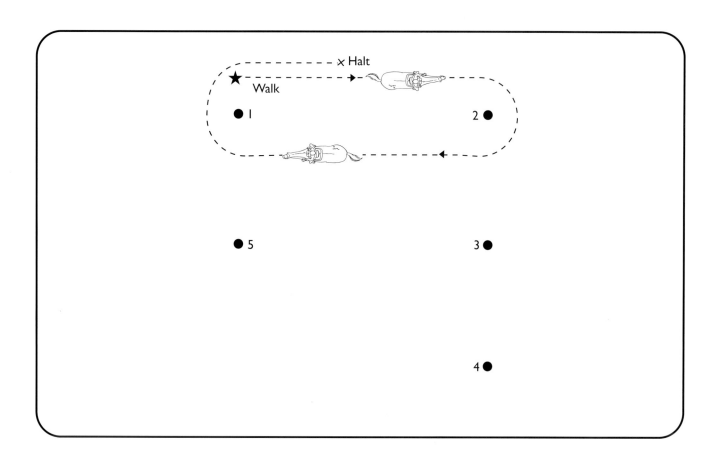

Step-by-Step

Practice with Two Hands

1. At Cone 1, pick up the walk, aiming toward Cone 2.

2. When your right foot is beside Cone 2, **lay the left rein on the horse's neck.** If he doesn't start to turn, nudge him with your inside leg at the cinch. Open the right rein, without any contact. You are neck reining right. ▶

3. Turn around Cone 2.

4. Walk back to Cone 1.

5. Neck rein right to turn around Cone 1.

6. Walk four more strides, and halt.

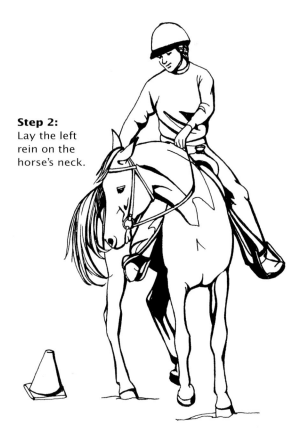

Step 2:
Lay the left rein on the horse's neck.

Switch to One Hand

1. **Pick up both reins in your left hand.** Bend your wrist so you hold your hand close to the saddle horn. **Hold your free hand forward, with fingers closed, in front of and above the pommel.** ▼

Step 1

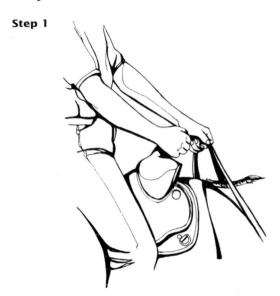

2. Resume the walk, and neck rein right to walk to Cone 5. Move your hand to the left so you lay the right rein on the horse's neck. Reinforce the rein with your inside leg at the cinch.

3. **Neck rein left around Cone 5,** and walk to Cone 3. ▼

Step 3

4. Neck rein left around Cone 3, and walk to Cone 2.

5. Neck rein left around Cone 2, and walk to Cone 1.

6. Neck rein left around Cone 1, and walk straight ahead.

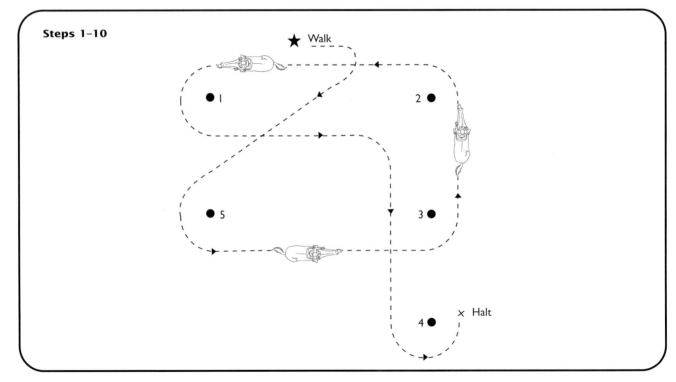

7. Neck rein right before nearing Cone 2. Walk to Cone 4.

8. Neck rein left around Cone 4.

9. Halt. Does your horse rein better to the left or the right?

10. Do a half-turn on the forehand to the right, using the neck rein. Lay the rein on the right side of the neck. Apply light calf pressure with your left leg. Your leg should apply a steady pressure, not on and off.

11. Walk past Cone 4.

12. Neck rein right.

13. Pick up the jog.

14. Jog a large circle around the five cones, neck reining at each corner. Try to turn close to Cones 1, 2, and 4.

15. Halt at Cone 4.

16. Repeat the neck reining at the walk, going in reverse order (steps 8 to 2).

17. Halt at Cone 5.

18. Do a half-turn on the forehand to the left. Use the right rein and right leg.

19. Halt and pet your horse.

Tips
- Think of lightness.
- If the horse leans on the neck rein, use the outside leg to correct.
- Reinforce with the leg aid.

Horse Sense
You can't pull harder with the neck rein. The horse must respond to the touch.

Challenge
- Alternate turning inside and outside the cones. Go around the outside of Cone 1, then the inside of Cone 2, and so on. Your horse will be less likely to anticipate your signal.
- Go back to lesson 2 on page 13, and try it using the neck rein at the walk and the jog.

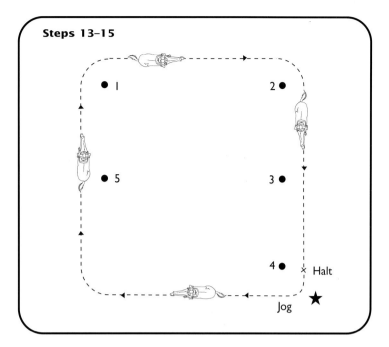

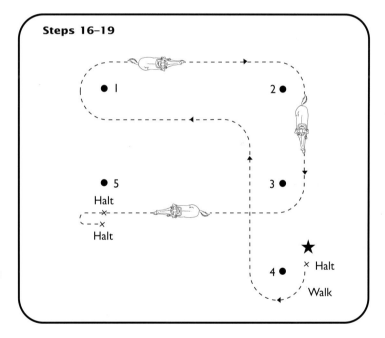

 Focus on Form

Don't use your leg too firmly in the turn on the forehand, or the horse will sidepass. Your rein steadies the forehand when you turn. Adjust rein pressure so the horse won't back up or walk more with the front feet. Keep your free hand relaxed so you don't look as if you're "two-handing" the horse.

Square-Cornered Circles

Does a circle have to be round? To help you improve your turns, California trainer Joe King's exercise transforms the circle into a series of square corners. You'll improve your eye and help your horse keep weight off his forehand. Think about keeping your horse upright while cornering so you won't overload the inside shoulder. You'll also get better at moving the horse's hip off your leg.

Objectives
- To walk and jog your horse through crisp turns
- To prepare your horse for the flying lead change

As you rein through turns, look for the horse to keep his shoulders up.

Benefits
- The horse will keep his shoulders up on his turns.
- Square corners will help to slow the horse.
- Forming a square corner will help the horse lope circles. He will be less likely to lean into the arc.

Time Frame — Medium

Setup
Place a single cone as your starting and ending point.

Step-by-Step

The Box
Envision how your box will look. Plan to walk four lines of six strides each. You'll start at the cone, and where will you end the first line? For a square, the other three lines will be dictated by the length and position of the first line. Avoid making any line a fence line.

1. From the cone, walk the first line of your box.

2. On the sixth stride, **use your legs to guide the horse in a 90-degree turn.** Your reins control the speed, while your legs control the direction. React first with your leg, so your hand can be still and soft. Keep your horse marching through the turn without losing rhythm. ▼

Step 2

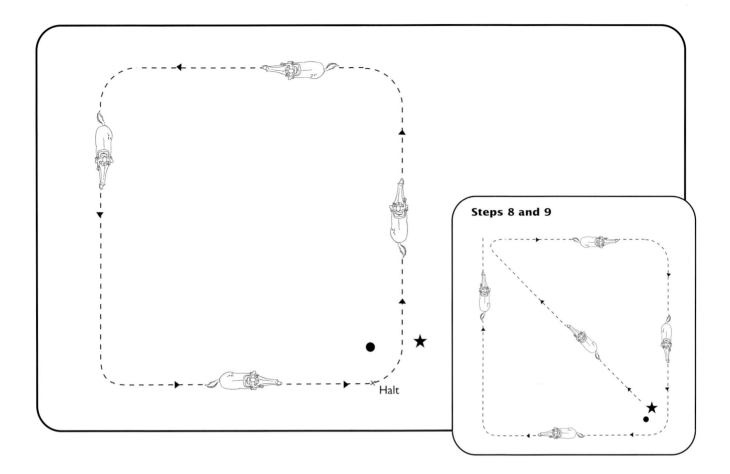

Steps 8 and 9

Halt

3. With your horse facing 90 degrees from the first line, walk the second line.

4. On the sixth stride, turn.

5. Walk the third line. You should be walking parallel to your first line.

6. On the sixth stride, turn. You should be lined up with the cone marking your starting point.

7. Walk to the cone and halt with your stirrup beside the cone. Did you form a perfect box? Did every turn match so your lines were straight?

8. Walk across the diagonal, to the spot where you made your second turn.

9. Repeat the box in the opposite direction. You should end diagonally across the box from the cone.

10. Repeat the pattern at the jog, increasing the strides from six to eight. The turns will come

faster when you increase your speed from the walk to the jog. Think ahead, and set your horse up for each turn.

Tips

- Keep the inside shoulder up.
- You guide with your leg so you're not hanging on the horse's face. Look for the horse to move from your leg and "stand up" in the turn.
- The sharp turns help the horse understand to drop his head and turn.
- Turns slow the horse faster, as you increase your speed. The horse will tend to slow down on his own.

Horse Sense

Don't overuse your hands so you oversteer your horse. You don't want to hang on the horse's face.

Challenge

Place a cone at each corner.

Variation: The Stair Steps

1. Walk forward four strides.

2. Cue the horse with your inside leg and outside rein to turn left. ▶

3. Walk four strides.

4. Cue to turn right. You've formed the first step.

5. Walk four strides.

6. Cue to turn left.

7. Walk four strides.

8. Cue to turn right. This forms the second step.

9. Walk four strides.

10. Cue to turn left.

11. Walk four strides and halt. You've completed the third step. Do a turn on the forehand, and then walk down the stair steps.

Step 2:
Cue the horse with your inside leg and outside rein to turn left.

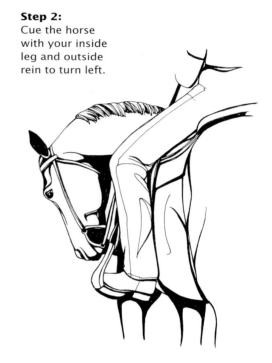

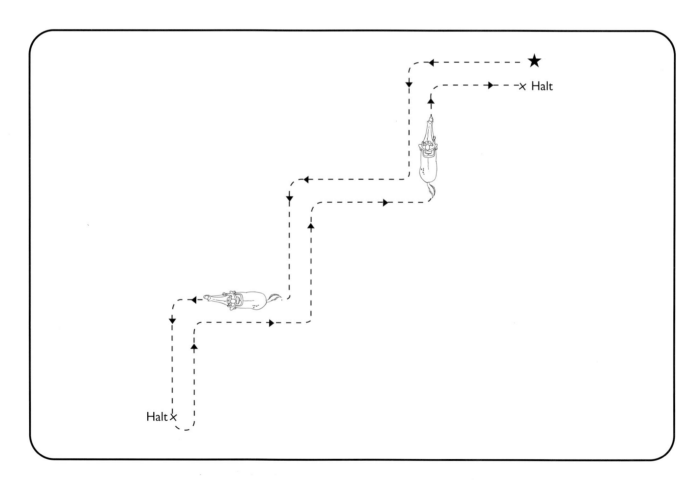

Refine Your Cues

Terry Berg is a champion reiner from Santa Fe, New Mexico. She teaches this pattern to nonprofessional riders, to help them ride straight lines and make turns on a green horse or a seasoned campaigner. Riding with spurs helps you refine your aids and control your leg. Think about the horse being so sensitive to your hand and leg that if you just think the movement, it will occur.

Objectives

- To guide every stride of the horse
- To analyze your horse's responses more closely
- To rein your horse the same, using either one or two hands on the reins
- To use your spurs in two ways

Benefit

Use this exercise as a warm-up. The simple questions you will pose to your horse will test his frame of mind that day.

Time Frame — Medium

Setup

A pen with square corners, with one cone near any side

When you lift your rein hand, your horse listens and responds.

Step-by-Step

1. Start at cone. Walk your horse along the rail of the pen, tracking left and riding with the reins in one hand.

2. Three strides before you reach the corner, turn left.

3. Walk around the pen. When you first pass the cone and approach the corner, listen to your horse. Does he start telling you where to turn? Tell him to go straight. Walk him deep into the corner.

4. Starting the fourth round, turn left on the diagonal. Listen to your horse. Does he start to drift toward the cone, or stay on the track you set? Tell him to go straight.

   This time, use your inside spur. **Reach back with your foot, behind the cinch, and scrape forward with the end of the spur, as shown below.** It should feel as if you're raking leaves with your spur, raking from back to front (behind the cinch to the back edge of the cinch). How does your horse respond to the spur? ▼

5. Turn left to aim at the cone.

6. Turn left to continue on the rail.

7. As you approach the spot where you first turned, before the corner, turn left on the diagonal.

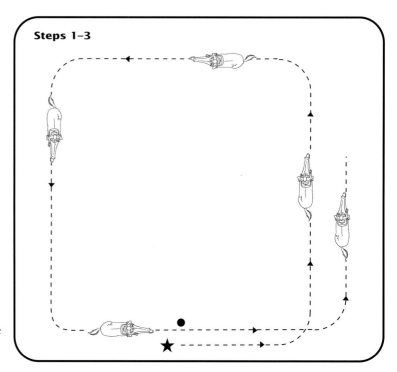

Steps 1–3

Step 4

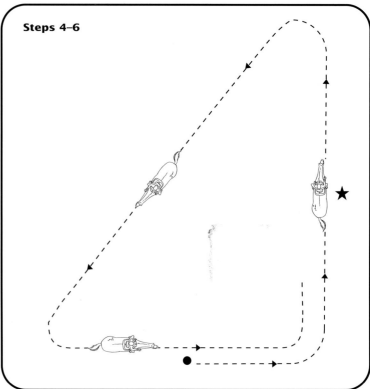

Steps 4–6

8. Walk straight, all the way to the rail.

9. Turn right and continue walking on the rail.

10. Say "whoa," and press your feet into the stirrups. Your feet or spurs should not contact the horse's sides.

11. Let your horse settle a moment at halt, then squeeze your calves for the walk.

12. Prepare to pick up the lope on the right lead. **Lift your hand slightly, and move it to the right.** Lean back, push with the outside leg, and "kiss" to your horse.

   If your horse tries to cut in when turning, or if he veers off the track, nudge or kick with the inside leg. Pick up your hand, use your leg, and lower your hand again. ▼

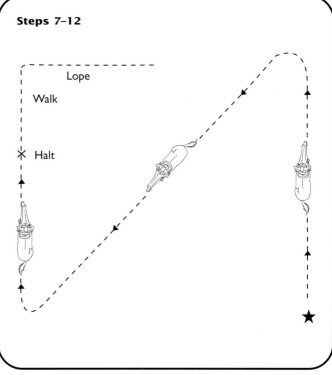

Steps 7–12

Lope

Walk

✕ Halt

Step 12

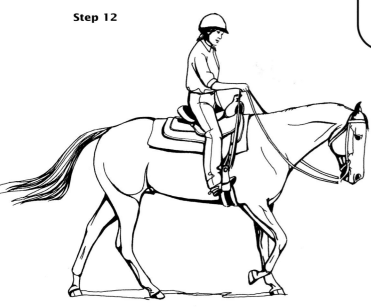

13. Drop down to the walk, and walk ten strides.

14. Again pick up the lope.

15. Feel your horse's willingness to stride forward actively. If you need to move him forward, squeeze every third stride.

   Your horse may respond better if you squeeze every fourth or fifth stride. You may need to touch him with the inside spur, or just squeeze with your calf.

16. Drop down to the walk, and halt.

Focus on Form

- Keep your rein hand down.
- As you apply your leg aid, stretch slightly back from the horse's withers. Don't sit forward.
- Feel control over your heel when you use your leg. Turn your toes out and press with the backs of your calves.
- Use the raking leaves motion with the spur instead of stabbing the horse. Your spur reaches an area measuring 2 by 4 inches (5 by 10 cm), behind the cinch. Be sure to rake and release, to give the horse relief and the opportunity to respond.

Tips

- Think about what you want your horse to do, and be precise about your signals.
- Your horse is aware of your hand position. Lift up your hand slightly to cue, then keep it down when you don't mean to cue. Your horse will learn that when you lift your hand, he's expected to respond.
- Practice the use of spurs, learning the rhythm of your foot motion. A tap may achieve the response you want.

Boxed In

The box — four poles placed to face the four directions of the map — is the focal point of this lesson. Colorado trainer Marge Brubaker describes a pattern to help you plan for crisper changes in gait. The three-part pattern tests your horse's readiness to react to your aids and helps you teach your horse to concentrate and wait for you. This lesson also introduces the simple lead change.

Objectives
- To test the horse's willingness to change gait and direction
- To achieve upward transitions more quickly
- To circle your horse more accurately

Benefits
- This pattern will help you follow a plan and ask for precise responses.
- Your horse will maintain his balance in transitions.

Time Frame — Medium

Setup
Four poles, arranged to form a box

A "box" formed from four poles gives you ample opportunity for different riding patterns.

Step-by-Step

The Walk and the Jog

1. Walk your horse in a straight line past the box.

2. Turn right.

3. Walk over both Poles N and S.

4. Turn left and walk a half-circle to aim back toward the box.

5. One stride from Pole S, pick up the jog.

6. Jog over Poles S and N.

7. Turn right and jog a three-quarter circle toward Pole E.

8. Jog over Poles E and W.

9. Turn right and jog a half-circle back toward Pole W.

10. Jog over Poles W and E. ▼

Step 10

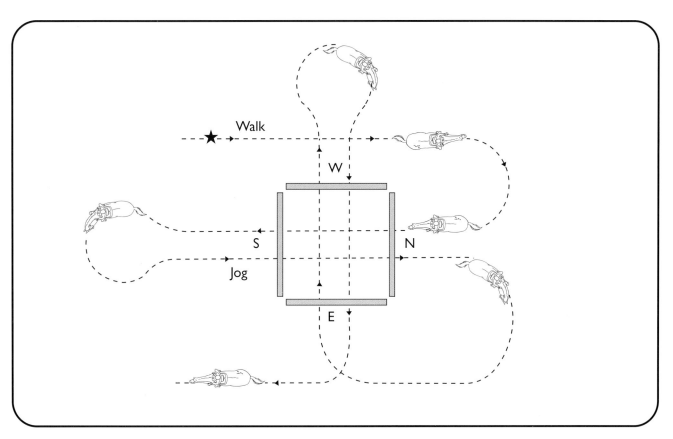

The Lope

1. One stride after you cross Pole E, pick up the lope on the right lead.

2. Lope a three-quarter circle toward Pole S.

3. Lope over Poles S and N.

4. One stride after you cross Pole N, ask for a simple change of lead. Drop to the trot for two strides, and pick up the left lead.

5. Turn left and lope a three-quarter circle toward Pole W.

6. Lope over Poles W and E.

7. Halt, and pet your horse.

Turn in the Box

1. Pick up the walk, and turn right to form a half-circle back toward Pole S.

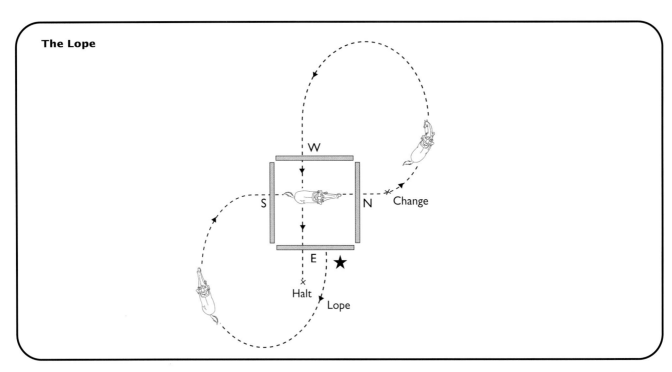

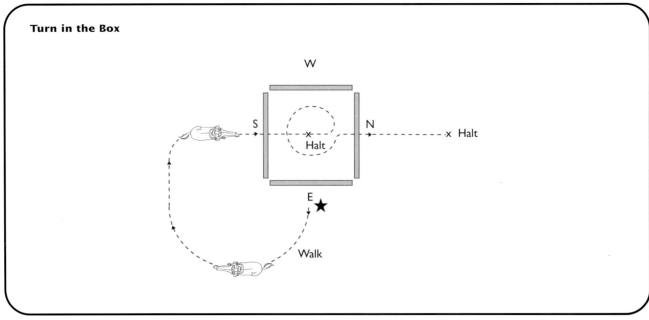

2. Walk over Pole S, and **halt with all four feet in the box.** ▼

Step 2

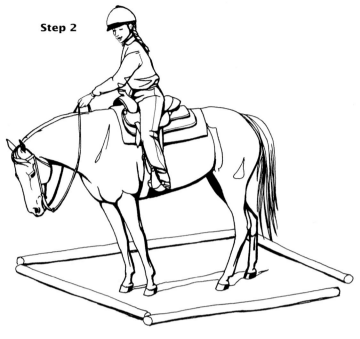

Tips

- Does your horse slow when you ask?
- On the lope-overs, one stride before you cross the first pole, push the horse forward or gather (collect) him.

Horse Sense

- Don't look down at the poles; keep your eyes straight ahead.
- Don't touch the rein to adjust the speed. You can throw off the horse's rhythm.

3. **Turn the horse left,** completely around in the box. **Stand up in the saddle,** and cluck to help the horse pick up his feet. You won't have enough room to do a turn on the forehand, so he will turn on both ends. ▼

Step 3

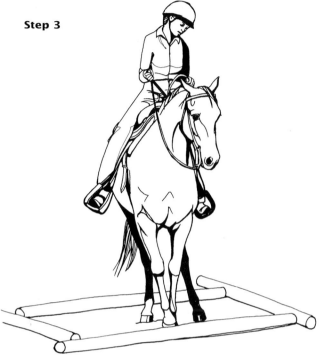

4. Walk over Pole N.

5. Halt, and pet your horse.

Chapter 4 Summary

Lessons in this chapter helped you to practice communication. You now understand the basics of how to ask your horse to listen to and respond to your signals. Ask yourself how your horse rates:

- Does he move in a steady, consistent manner, with gait, attitude, speed, headset, mouth, and tail?
- Does he feel more attentive to you?
- Does he work until you say stop?
- Does he move freely forward at a comfortable speed?
- Does he move with an invisible connection to you, with or without rein contact?

Now look at yourself:

- Do you think positively about starting an exercise?
- Do you tell your horse what you want him to do — not what he's not to do?

You'll expand upon this knowledge in chapter 5. With your horse heeding your cues, you'll ask him to move with more impulsion, with energy from the hindquarters.

The horse loping with impulsion demonstrates fluid, forward energy. He maintains balance because he engages the hindquarters.

chapter 5

Impulsion

To perform Western riding maneuvers, your horse needs to move with impulsion. He actively propels himself forward, and he feels light and energetic — never heavy or "dead." A Western horse never moves with the animation of a gaited horse or a dressage competitor, but he is still lively and expressive.

Ideally, your horse sprints and turns by engaging the hindquarters. His hind legs reach deep underneath his body. He propels himself forward from behind, so he comes through. He is able to "round" his back, or hold his spine up without hollowing the back. To lope slowly in a true three-beat gait, he needs impulsion.

From practicing lessons in the previous chapters, you started thinking about your horse's balance. Your horse should feel that he's moving forward from your leg. This series of lessons will focus more on refining the motion and on how your horse carries himself.

You will practice moving your horse from the hip. The lessons in this chapter will help you encourage your horse to drive forward to his face, still keeping an even tempo without rushing. As you develop and recognize impulsion, you're working up to collection, where you shorten or compress your horse for demanding maneuvers.

As you think more about the quality of movement, pay close attention to each stride. Concentrate on improving your communication and on how you connect with your horse.

Listen more closely to your horse as you ask him for more intense work. Look for one ear swiveled back to you. A horse that's paying attention to you will consistently keep an ear on you.

These lessons increase the degree of difficulty. You're going to apply your aids more frequently, posing questions to your horse. In response, you expect precise answers. If you're not sure your horse responded, ask again. (He probably didn't.) Reward him for giving you the outcome you anticipate — praise him with voice, a lighter seat, or a pet.

The maneuvers in this chapter present exams that test how your horse works. Ask yourself, does he move in balance consistently? Does he move readily, or do you sense a momentary resistance? When you ask for a tight turn, what response does he give you? As the difficulty escalates, you and your horse will make mistakes. Have a game plan, so you know what you ask and can predict how your horse reacts. Be ready to address what might happen. You won't want to visualize an error, but be ready to halt an exercise, run through a mental checklist, and possibly try an alternate approach.

What if you make a mistake? The horse doesn't know you told him something wrong. Concentrate on what you tell him and on how he reacts.

Turn on the Haunches

In slow motion, this maneuver helps your horse to engage the hindquarters. His hind legs carry his weight, and he'll place his hind legs under himself more. To help you position your horse, the exercise progresses through three locations. And after you've practiced the third variation, test your skill by asking for the turn on the haunches, then the forehand, then the sidepass — all variations of lateral movement.

Objectives

▪ To do a half-turn on the haunches, moving the forehand in 180 degrees of a circle
▪ To complete the figure without your horse moving forward or back with his hind feet

▪ To help your horse shift his weight back on the haunches

Benefits

▪ Moving one step at a time will help you and your horse slow down. You will coordinate your aids in slow motion.
▪ This exercise will help the horse carry more weight on the hindquarters.

Time Frame — Medium

Setup — A pen or arena

Your hips, legs, and rein help the horse shift his weight onto the haunches.

Step-by-Step

Turn in the Corner

1. Back your horse into a corner of the pen or arena, so he stands at an angle to the fence line on your left and right.

2. Press with your right leg to make your horse move the forehand toward the fence to your left. Your leg will transfer the weight back to ask him to turn on the hindquarters. You should feel the horse arc in response, shifting the weight back from your leg. Pick him up with your hand, using the indirect (outside) rein to push his shoulders over.

Correctly bend your horse in the turn, and maintain the rhythm and sequence of footfalls. Feel the foreleg cross in front of the opposite leg.

3. As your horse steps to the left, continue to cue for the next step. You may have to press your leg for each step, releasing pressure as you feel him yield. Your horse may complete the half-turn in two or three steps.

4. When you are lined up parallel to the fence line, halt and pet. Count to 10 while your horse settles.

5. Next, turn to the right. Press with your left leg. Does your horse turn more readily in this direction?

6. Halt and pet when you're parallel to the other fence line.

7. Jog your horse away from the corner. Always follow a slow, controlled maneuver with free, forward movement.

Alternate Approach

Isolate the horse's rear end, putting his nose in the corner and moving him one step left, pausing, then one step right.

Steps 1–3

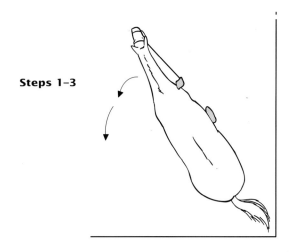

Step 4

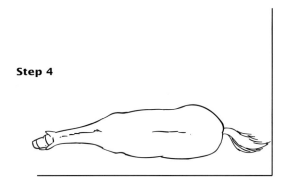

Step 5

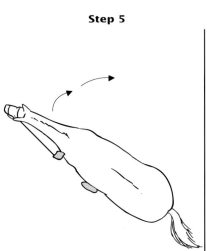

Step 7

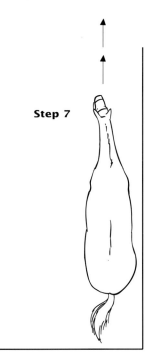

Turn on the Fence

1. Circle left. Form three large circles, jogging left. ▼

Step 1

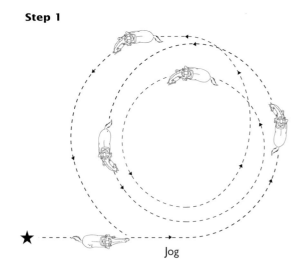

Jog

2. Pick up the lope, and lope ten strides parallel to the fence line. Halt. ▼

Step 2

Lope   Halt

3. Ask for a turn on the haunches to the left, aiming to end up facing the corner where you started the lesson. ▼

Step 3

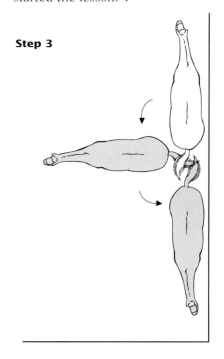

4. Walk forward ten strides.

5. Halt. Ask for a turn on the haunches to the right. In which direction does your horse turn more readily?

Tips

- Look for the horse to anchor his hind foot, so it doesn't move.
- He should step over his pivot foot.
- He should not cross the legs behind one another.
- He should drop the hip, without sticking it out to the side.
- As your horse becomes attuned to your cues, aim to cue him with your hip. Your weight shift can signal him to move the forehand.
- Remember to let your horse relax by moving freely forward.

 Focus on Form

Sit up straight. Watch how you use the reins.

Turn in the Pen

1. Away from the fence line, walk your horse on a straight line.

2. Halt.

3. Ask for a half-turn on the haunches, moving first in your horse's weaker direction.

4. Walk forward ten strides.

5. Check your horse, asking him to halt and at the same time asking him to turn on the haunches.
    You're asking him to turn in his stronger direction, so you increase the likelihood of a successful turn from the walk.

Horse Sense

■ Many horses will try to swing the hindquarters and walk out of the turn. Don't let your horse walk forward to evade the movement.

■ Don't rush your horse, or he may try to escape. Avoid pressuring him so he "locks up."

■ A major disobedience is the horse pushing against your leg. He should not move backward or forward but sweep to the side.

■ If your horse resists, use your rein end as a whip. Hold your hand out to the side and slap the leather on the horse's flank, behind the leg you're using as the cue.

■ Some trainers discourage riders from using a fence as a mechanical aid. Be sure to practice this maneuver in an open area, to teach your horse to depend on himself. If you have trouble visualizing where to start and stop, you can draw a line in the dirt as an invisible fence.

Challenge

The "Whirling Walk" lesson on page 115 builds on this exercise. Pay attention to what you do with your hip as you start to cue for the turn.

Walk your horse on a circle. Gather your horse to you and ask him to change directions from the walk. You'll "sweep" his front end, looking for him to step over and move his forehand while planting his inside hind foot.

Outside Rein Rhythm

Whenever you ride a pattern, think about your impulsion. Does your horse feel more "alive" going toward the gate? Does he feel "dead" going away from the barn? The frequent changes of direction will test your reining, and also how your horse adjusts his balance as he starts and completes a turn. Use the break between "forward" and "reverse" as a checkpoint to replay your performance.

The outside rein guides the horse, maintaining the forward energy into the direction you set.

Objectives

- To practice transitions on the diagonal track, relying on the outside rein
- To keep the horse's rhythm through frequent changes of direction
- To test your horse's impulsion by riding him in a consistent frame, speed, and direction
- To use your leg to move the horse and your rein to turn the horse
- To ride on the outside rein
- To ride in the half-seat over a single pole or sets of poles

Benefits

- Your horse will carry you forward consistently.
- Your horse will keep his impulsion when slowing, working toward the beginnings of collection.
- Your horse will respond to the outside rein as the dominating rein.

Time Frame — Long

Setup

An area at least 100 feet (30 m) square. Arrange five poles, as shown opposite.

Step-by-Step

Trot freely in a large circle before starting this pattern. Feel your horse's balance. Is he strung out, or heavy on the forehand? Push forward with your inside leg, so you feel him move on the outside rein. Ask him to relax the jaw. You should feel him move in better balance, from back to front, before continuing this lesson.

Forward

1. Pick up the lope on the right lead.

2. Lope between Poles 1 and 3, and turn left in a half-circle.

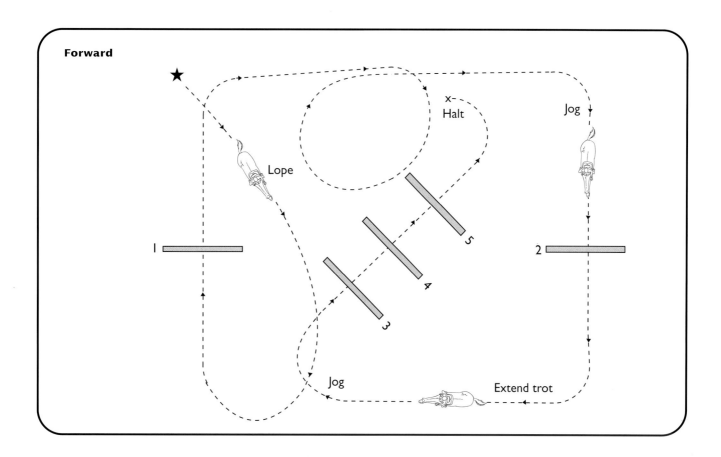

Forward

★ · · · · Lope

Halt x- -

Jog ↓

1 ▮▮▮

2 ▮▮▮

3 ▮▮▮ 4 ▮▮▮ 5 ▮▮▮

Jog Extend trot

3. Use your outside rein, inside leg to help round the horse, so he doesn't lope on his forehand. You want to encourage him to lope with his hind legs reaching underneath himself, without speeding him up.

4. Lope toward Pole 1, and lope over it.

5. Turn right.

6. Lope a large circle to the right. Use the end of Pole 4 as the outer boundary of your circle. Drive the horse with your outside leg, and supple him to your inside leg. Feel your horse move on the outside rein as you push with the inside leg. When you turn your inside toe out and heel in, feel the horse give his rib cage to you. ▶

7. Turn right, and plan for the downward transition past the corner. Use your inside rein to bend the horse slightly to the inside, and soften the response you anticipate.

Step 6:
Lope a large circle to the right.

8. Slow to the jog, softly. Did your horse remain in balance as he moved from the lope to the jog?

9. Jog over Pole 2, and turn right.

10. When you straighten after the turn, **ask the horse to extend into a long trot.** Either post or stand in the stirrups, holding onto the saddle horn.

Encourage your horse to reach his legs underneath him by squeezing with both legs. If you can, squeeze with your upper leg, without forcing yourself up from the saddle. ▼

Step 10

 Focus on Form

- Your horse should feel strong and elastic through his joints, and so should you. As you jog, sit comfortably in the saddle while you "sit tall." Bring your shoulders back, and feel them sit slightly behind the point of your hips (the front of the pelvis).
- In transitions, stay tall in the saddle. Your horse's movements shouldn't jar you loose.

11. Slow the horse's stride back to the jog as you approach Pole 3.

12. Turn right, aiming to the middle of the line of three poles.

13. Keep your legs on the horse's sides with gentle calf pressure as you near Pole 3. Your horse may try to break his rhythm over the poles.

14. Rise into the half-seat. Keep your legs in place and your feet steady as you "float" over the seat of your saddle. Let your hands slide forward slightly, and keep them independent from the action of your lower body.

15. Jog over Poles 3, 4, and 5. Did your horse pick up his feet over the poles?

16. Softly settle back down into your saddle. Turn left, and halt near the end of Pole 5. Pet your horse. Did you maintain your rhythm over the poles, without losing your balance? Did you remember to use the outside rein to turn left after the poles?

Reverse

1. Do a half-turn on the haunches, so you see Pole 5 on your right. You'll now repeat the exercise in the reverse direction.

2. Pick up the jog, turning right to line up for another jog over the three poles.

3. Again, set your rhythm in the approach, and rise into the half-seat.

4. Jog over Poles 5, 4, and 3.

5. Turn left.

6. Extend the trot between Pole 1 and the turn toward Pole 2. Do you stay in control when you want to speed up?

7. Drop back to the jog one stride before the turn toward Pole 2.

8. Jog over Pole 2.

9. One stride after Pole 2, pick up the left lead.

10. Turn left.

11. Circle left.

12. Turn left, toward Pole 1.

13. Lope over Pole 1. ▼

Step 13

14. Turn left, and form a half-circle back to the original starting point.

15. Halt, and pet your horse.

Tips

■ When you put your legs on the horse, he should respond to a light leg.

■ Feel that your horse turns and stays in balance as you guide him.

■ Feel your horse lean slightly into the outside rein, as you push with your inside leg.

Horse Sense

■ Does the horse slow down when you want to go forward without stopping?

■ Don't let your horse jar you upward in a transition. If he feels strung out, moving too heavily on the forehand, circle him. Bend the horse and keep him moving. You can help the horse find his balance point, which may not necessarily be flexing.

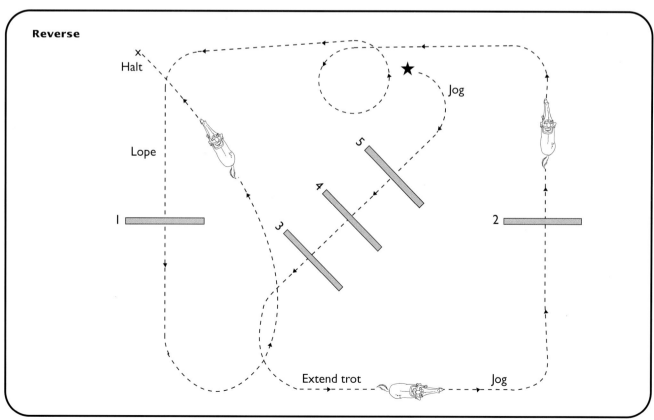

lesson 25
Sidewinder

Even if you ride a finished horse, you're always training the animal. Lateral exercises such as the Sidewinder help your horse maintain his rhythm and impulsion, while remaining supple and responsive. At the walk, trot, and lope, you're also challenged to check your position constantly and adjust your aids as you follow the pattern. (The Sidewinder is also known as the leg yield, an exercise used in the dressage discipline.)

The horse yields to your signals, bending away from the direction he moves.

Objectives
- To move the horse right and left while also going forward
- To encourage the horse to free up the shoulders
- To use lateral aids of rein and leg
- To apply the indirect rein and outside leg
- To move the horse in the leg yield exercise

Benefits
- Like the sidepass, this exercise will make your horse more flexible and lighter in the forehand. You confirm the horse's willingness to respond to your leg cues.
- The horse gives with nose, shoulder, and rib cage.
- The horse carries more weight on the hindquarters.
- The horse maintains the tempo of the gait and keeps his body straight.
- When the horse moves laterally, to the side, you increase your control and your confidence. The leg yield helps control an exuberant horse, channeling his energy.

Time Frame — Long

Setup
A pen (you'll be using fence lines as visual boundaries), with five cones available for loping

Step-by-Step

Sidewinder at the Walk

1. Walk the horse forward, not too close to the fence line.

2. Ask him to move over to the right, so he crosses over like a sidepass as he walks. Press with the left (inside) leg so you push the horse into your right hand. Use your leg and hand at the same time. The indirect right rein helps the horse pick up his shoulder. Move your left rein out to the side, with light contact. Your right leg remains in light contact at the cinch.

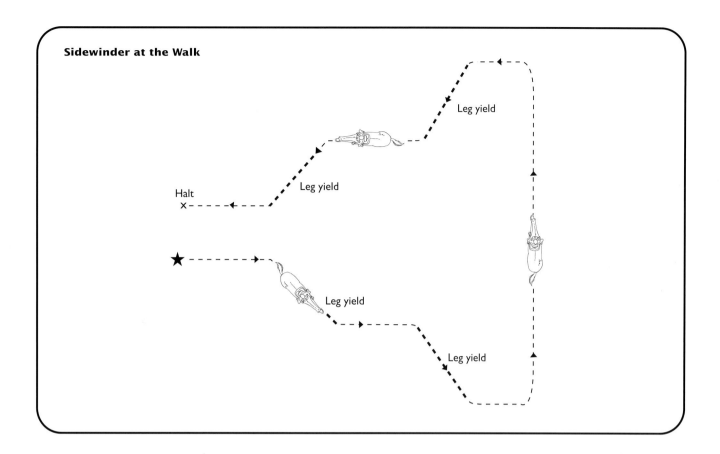

Sidewinder at the Walk

Halt

Leg yield

Leg yield

Leg yield

Leg yield

You should feel the horse give with his nose as you move the shoulders laterally. He is bent away from the direction he moves, but his body is parallel to the fence line. Squeeze and release the left leg with every stride. Your leg moves the hip over. Aim to maintain a regular rhythm and a consistent angle. ▼

Step 2

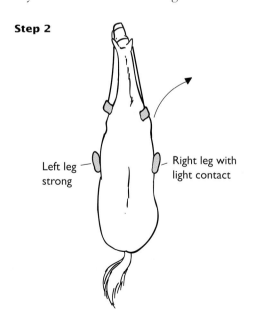

Left leg strong

Right leg with light contact

3. Move the horse to the right for five strides. Check that your horse keeps his body parallel to the rail. Glance forward to check the bend. You should see the nose bent slightly to the left as he moves to the right, so you can see his left eye and nostril.

4. Straighten the horse for ten strides.

5. Repeat the leg yield.

6. Straighten and walk to the corner.

7. Turn left, and walk along the rail.

8. Turn left again, and walk straight for ten strides.

9. Press your right leg and move your right rein out to the side. Feel the horse move to the left for five strides; look for his right eye and nostril.

10. Straighten the horse for five strides.

11. Repeat the leg yield. Walk straight 5 strides.

12. Halt and pet your horse. Let him relax with forward motion.

Sidewinder at the Trot

1. Turn right, and pick up the jog.

2. Leg yield right for eight strides. Cue in rhythm to the trotting stride. Think "left-two, left-two" as you squeeze with the gait.

3. Jog straight forward for four strides.

4. Halt.

5. Walk and do a half-circle to the right.

6. Pick up the long trot.

7. Leg yield left for eight strides. ▶

8. Slow to a jog for four strides, straight forward.

9. Halt.

10. Reverse and repeat the pattern in the opposite direction.

11. Slow to the walk, and walk large circles around the pen.

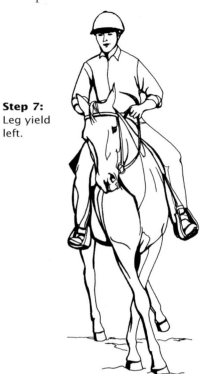

Step 7: Leg yield left.

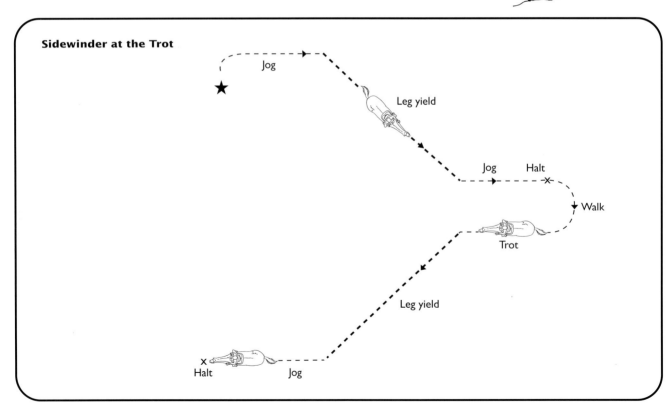

Sidewinder at the Trot

Jog

Leg yield

Jog   Halt

Walk

Trot

Leg yield

Halt   Jog

Sidewinder in the Figure 8

1. Resume the walk, circling left in the first large circle of a figure 8. Complete the first circle in the walk.

2. Leg yield two steps right to start the second circle. Feel your horse pushing off from the inside. Complete the second circle in the walk.

3. Leg yield two steps left.

4. Pick up the jog, and do another figure 8. Leg yield at both junctions.

5. Repeat at the long trot, forming two larger circles.

6. Slow to the walk, and let your horse relax by walking around the pen on a loose rein.

Alternate Approach

Your horse might move less readily from one leg. Concentrate on that leg by doing a half-circle to change direction.

For the right leg:

1. Walk straight.

2. Leg yield to the left for eight strides.

3. Half-circle to the right, forming a horseshoe.

4. At the end of the shoe, again leg yield to the left for eight strides.

Challenge

Do all steps for the alternate approach on a loose rein, using the neck rein.

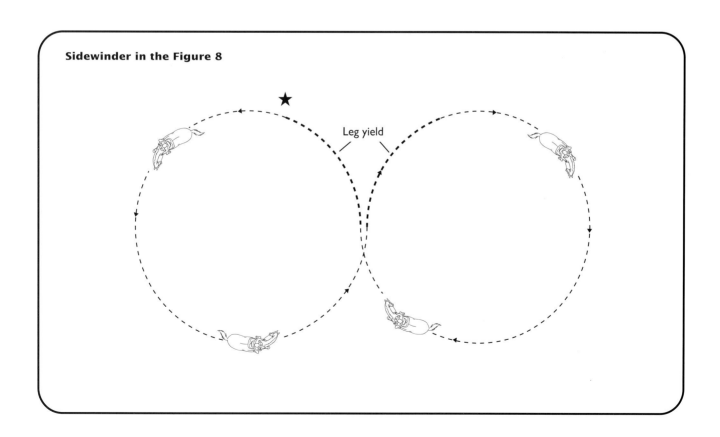

Sidewinder in the Figure 8

Leg yield

Sidewinder in the Lope

In this variation, you use the leg yield to prepare your horse for a lead change. You'll perform a simple lead change in the figure 8 pattern.

1. Lope the first circle of a figure 8 twice.

2. Halt. Leg yield at walk.

3. Pick up the other lead, and lope the second circle twice.

4. Halt. Leg yield at walk.

5. Repeat, with leg yield at the jog.

6. Set up a line of five cones.

7. **Lope through the cones** with the simple change. ▼

Step 7

Tips

▪ Look for the head to bend first, then the shoulder and the rib cage.
▪ If the horse resists bending in the leg yield, increase leg pressure. You may have to bump him with your heel, or use your spur.
▪ The horse should move lightly on the shoulder.
▪ The horse may not respond to the pressure of your leg pressing his side and may start to lose his forward motion or drift off track. Correct either evasion at the stride where it begins.
▪ Avoid constant pressure with your cues. Reward the horse by releasing pressure as he steps to the side.

Horse Sense

▪ Follow lateral motion with forward motion. Loosen the reins and let the horse walk or jog freely.
▪ Your leg moves the hip over. Don't try to "crank" the horse over with the rein.
▪ Don't allow your horse to "escape" either left or right. Keep an equal amount of pressure on both reins.
▪ Keep the horse straight. The horse shouldn't lead with his shoulder or fall over (lean) into the shoulder.
▪ Don't allow the horse to fall over with his shoulders. If he starts this, try a turn on the forehand first to get his weight more on the haunches. Then move the haunches first and "hold" the shoulders up.
▪ Maintain the rhythm of the walk and the trot. Avoid keeping your leg constantly on the horse. Think of using your leg like your fist in a punching bag — squeeze, release, squeeze, release.

Snake River Serpentines

More serpentines — those snaky loops and straight lines demand a plan and an eye for what's next in the pattern. This lesson's two segments test you and your horse for shifts in impulsion. In riding, sometimes you want to move forward with energy; other times you seek a more relaxed pace. These serpentines also introduce you to the counter canter — improving your horse's balance by intentionally loping on the "wrong" lead.

Objectives

- To combine the arcs of the serpentine with degrees of impulsion
- To move your horse from animation to tranquillity, shifting up and down

- To discern the difference between pace and energy
- To recognize and deal with opposition to what you ask

Benefits

- Your horse will move with suppleness and impulsion.
- You'll vary collecting your horse, asking him to be animated at a slower pace, with inviting him to "die" at a faster pace. This pattern helps relax a hot or fresh horse.

Time Frame — Medium

Setup — Arrange three cones, set 20 feet (6 m) apart.

In the countercanter, you lope toward one direction on the opposite lead.

Step-by-Step

Forward

1. From a walk, pick up a lively trot. You don't want a fast, on the forehand trot, but a purposeful, rhythmic gait.

2. One stride before asking for a turn to the right, slow to a jog. Deepen your seat.

3. Jog right to form the first loop.

4. Move back into the trot, trotting to the left of Cone 3.

5. One stride before asking for the turn left, slow back to the jog.

6. Jog left to form the second loop.

7. Jog three strides.

8. As you pass to the right of Cone 2, turn left to form a small circle. Ride the circle with Cone 2 in the center.

   Keep your horse between your reins and your legs. Your outside rein turns his body, while your inside rein keeps him bent to the inside. ▼

Step 8

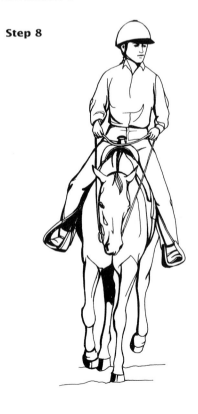

9. As you complete the circle, pick up the lope on the right lead.

10. Lope right to form the third loop.

11. Lope past Cone 1; Cone 1 should be on your right.

12. Slow to the jog.

13. Jog three strides, and slow to the walk.

14. Turn right and halt. Pet your horse and let him settle.

Reverse

1. Turn your horse around, in a half-turn on the haunches, so Cone 1 is to your left.

2. Walk forward ten strides and turn left. You should be about six strides past Cone 1.
   You'll be picking up the counter canter, so you need to plan a wide, sweeping turn.

3. Ask your horse to pick up the right lead.

4. You'll **make a wide sweeping turn on the counter canter.** As you approach the turn, feel your inside rein to keep the horse's head to the inside. Your right leg and right hand hold him up to the outside to maintain his strides on the counter canter. Your left leg keeps him bent to the inside. ▼

Step 4

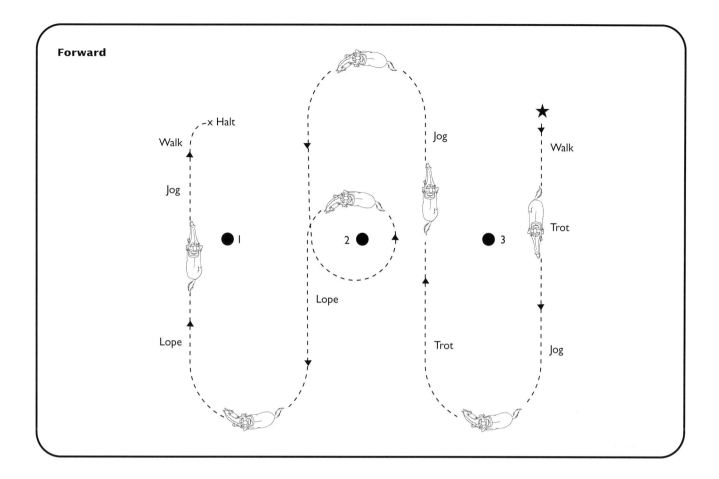

5. Keep your horse on the counter canter for three strides, and then drop to the jog.

6. Jog two strides, and then ask for the left lead the rest of the way around the turn.

7. As you pass Cone 2, on your right, drop back to the jog.

8. Repeat the rest of the serpentine pattern in reverse.

Horse Sense

Don't allow your horse to cut the turns when you change direction. Keep your loops the same size, and make the third loop align with the first one.

Tips

■ In this pattern, think of your horse flowing like a river, quiet then rapid.

■ Can you achieve different energies in different phases?

■ How do you keep your horse's bend and balance in the transitions? You want your maneuvers to look planned and thoughtful, not hurried.

■ Be sure to make a wide turn on the counter canter. This exercise challenges the horse's balance.

Coiled Mecate

Like the spirals of the horsehair reins of the mecate, this pattern flows in a series of circles. You've practiced arcs and flexions, and now you are test bending with a consistent rhythm and impulsion on a series of concentric circles. Adjust the bend to curve as circles become smaller, and aim for an unchanging speed. Look to the center of the circles so your body cues your horse.

Objectives

- To maintain impulsion on circles of different sizes, each smaller than the previous circle
- To ride your horse in five circles of descending size, all of the same shape

Benefit

Your horse will keep his rhythm and energy on the circle. While bent on an arc, he'll continue moving forward at the speed you set.

Time Frame — Short

Setup

A large area, ideally at least 80 feet (24 m) square. Tape or mark numbers, from 1 to 5, on two sides of five cones. Arrange the five cones 10 feet (3 m) apart in a line, as shown opposite. You should be able to see the numbers from both the north and south sides of the figure.

Bend your horse at the walk, with the bend appropriate to the size of the circle.

Step-by-Step

1. Walk to the right of Cone 1, and halt with the cone beside your left stirrup. Look left to site the five cones.

2. At Cone 1, walk left to begin the large circle that you'll end at Cone 2.

3. At the midpoint of the first circle (halfway complete), look across to see Cone 2.

4. In the last quarter of your first circle, position your horse so you'll walk between Cones 1 and 2.

5. Passing Cone 2 (to your left), start the next circle.

6. Complete this second circle between Cones 2 and 3.

7. Continue circling left so you form a spiral toward Cone 5. Keep the horse's rhythm the same on all spirals. **Feel the outside thrust on small circles.** ▼

Step 7

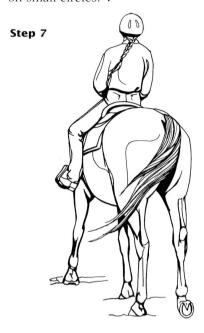

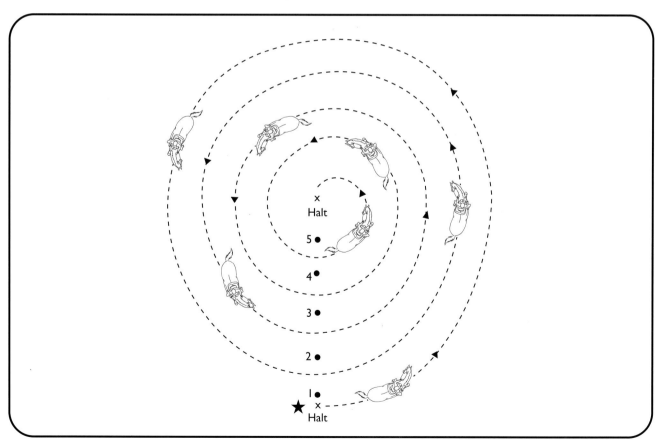

8. Halt facing Cone 5. Evaluate each circle. Was it round? Or was it a rectangle, an oval, or a polygon?

9. Do a half-turn on the haunches, to face away from Cone 5. ▼

Step 9

10. Retrace your steps in the same number of spirals, out toward Cone 1.

Tip

Ask, where did your horse "suck back," or lose impulsion?

Horse Sense

Your horse may try to cut in on a circle. Aim to keep circles uniform and round.

Challenge

- Repeat the figure using only the neck rein.
- Add a small circle around each cone. Start by circling left around Cone 1, then a large circle to Cone 2. Circle left around Cone 2, and continue. ▼

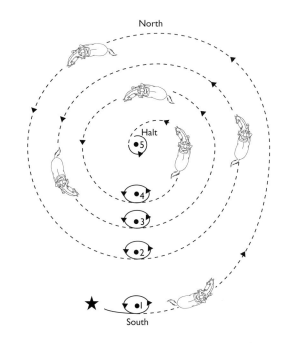

Dallas Diagonal

Diagonal lines across the arena keep your horse alert. Moving corner to corner breaks up the sameness of "on-the-rail," especially when you add transitions. Use the cones as signposts, and watch your turns. Keep your impulsion constant as you approach and negotiate changes in direction. As you plan and execute upward and downward transitions, you should feel your horse shift his weight on his haunches.

Objectives

- To guide the horse and maintain activity through jog/trot/lope transitions
- To practice lengthening and shortening your horse
- To recognize and maintain impulsion during changes in speed and direction

Benefits

- Transitions on the diagonal will help develop your eye.
- More exact demands will sharpen your horse's responses.

Time Frame — Medium

Setup

Arrange four cones, as shown on next page. Space Cones 1, 2, and 3 about 10 feet (3 m) apart. Cone 4 should be about 40 feet (12 m) from Cone 3.

On patterns, maintain rhythm and relaxation along with impulsion. Forward energy doesn't demand increased speed.

Step-by-Step

Part 1

1. Starting to the left of Cone 4, pick up the long trot. Extend your horse's gait, using your inside leg.

2. At the corner, turn right and slow to the jog. Use your outside rein to turn the horse. Slow the horse, but maintain his rhythm.

3. Jog toward Cone 2, across the diagonal. Pass Cone 2 on your right.

4. Jog straight for four strides.

5. Liven up your horse, and pick up the long trot as you turn toward Cone 3. Pass Cone 3 on your right.

6. Slow to the jog as you approach Cone 4; Cone 4 will be on your right.

Part 2

1. Jog four strides.

2. Pick up the lope, on the right lead.

3. **Turn right in a half-circle** so you're loping toward Cone 3. ▼

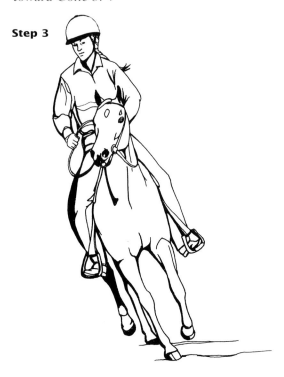

Step 3

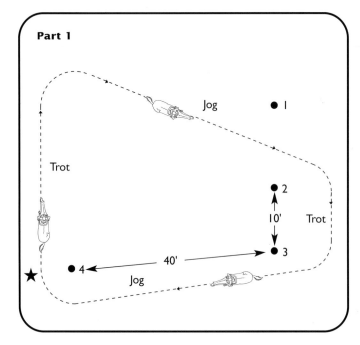

Part 1

Jog

● 1

Trot

● 2

10'

Trot

40'

● 3

● 4

Jog

★

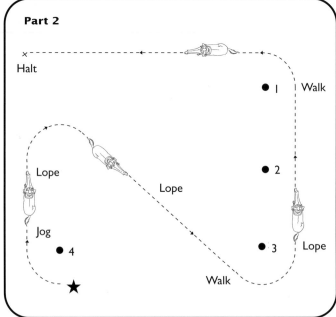

Part 2

× Halt

● 1 Walk

Lope

Lope

● 2

Jog

● 4

● 3 Lope

Walk

★

4. Pass Cone 3 on your left. Two strides before the corner, drop to the walk.

5. Turn left.

6. Pick up the lope on the left lead. Check that your horse departs crisply from the walk and that he lopes straight.

7. As you pass Cone 2, off to your left, guide your horse toward Cone 1. Pass Cone 1 on your left.

8. Lope straight.

9. Two strides before the corner, drop to the walk.

10. Turn left and walk to the corner. Halt.

Part 3

1. Pick up the jog, aiming toward Cone 2. Pass it on your right.

2. Jog straight to the fence.

3. Turn left.

4. One stride after the turn, **pick up the lope on the left lead.** ▶

5. Lope a half-circle to the left so you're loping straight across the diagonal toward Cone 4.

6. Halt at Cone 4.

Tips

■ Think rhythm and bend.

■ Keep checking the amount of activity your horse shows. Where does he lose his impulsion?

Horse Sense

Your horse may start drifting on turns in this pattern. Visualize the perfect turn, and correct him immediately if he wobbles. Correct him in the stride where he starts to drift.

Step 4:
Pick up the lope on the left lead.

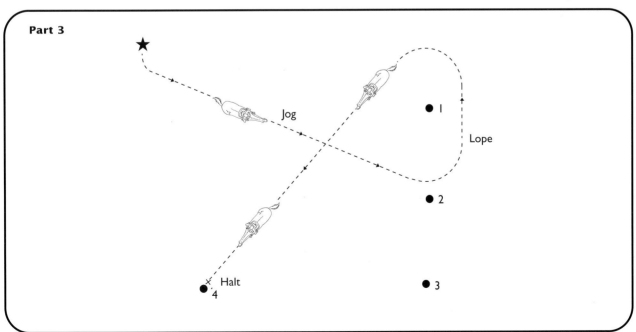

lesson 29

Stop on Your Butt

Colorado reining trainers Terry Wegener and Guy Vernon advocate these exercises to keep your horse soft and flexible. Even if you never try the reining event, your horse should stop on his hindquarters from any gait. A slow-motion rollback helps him "sit down," or rock back on his haunches. Teaching him to back up after the stop keeps him ready for your follow-up request. Remember your "whoa," and keep your rein hand down and soft.

Objectives

- To encourage the horse to stop on the hindquarters
- To tell your horse "whoa," and he backs up.
- To feel your horse stop softly, staying flexible instead of resisting you.

Benefits

- The horse will shift his weight back, engaging the hindquarters. He will use the most powerful part of his body, the hindquarters, to stop.

- This response and position will prepare him for the sliding stop, which you will use if you plan to show in reining events.

Time Frame — Medium

Setup — Along a fence line or a wall

Step-by-Step

Stop at the Fence

1. Walk the horse along the fence line or wall.

2. Bend the horse left, into the fence, with your inside leg and rein.

3. Say "whoa," and feel the horse "sit down." Drive him with your legs to push his hindquarters further under him and to keep the shoulders up.

4. Rock back in the saddle as you drive with your legs.

Hindquarters down and shoulders up! When you stop, your horse rocks back, ready for your signal to stand or turn.

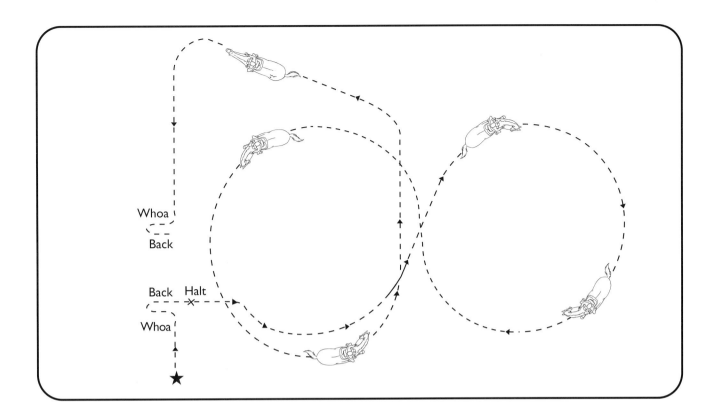

5. Use your legs to bump the horse, and back him up two steps away from the fence. Don't allow him to turn left or right, but hold him straight with the reins so he has to back up. ▼

6. Halt, and let the horse settle.

7. Turn away from the fence and walk a large figure 8 on a loose rein.

8. Aim back toward the fence. Turn left and now walk toward your starting point.

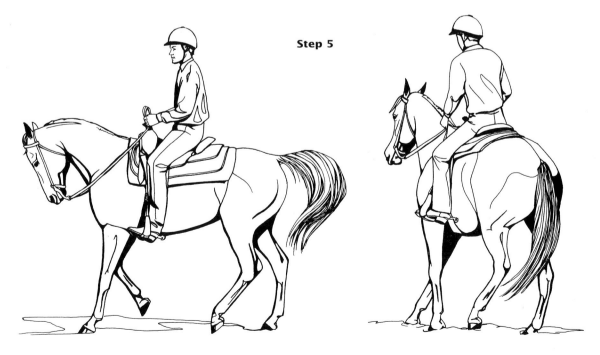

Step 5

9. Bend horse right, into the fence, with your inside leg and rein. Repeat Steps 3 thorough 6.

Stop in the Pen

1. Walk in a large circle away from the fence.

2. Say "whoa," and rock back. Pick up the rein to feel the horse yield. **Bump with your legs to cue the horse to back up.** You should feel the horse dropping his hindquarters, pushing into the ground. ▼

Steps 1–3

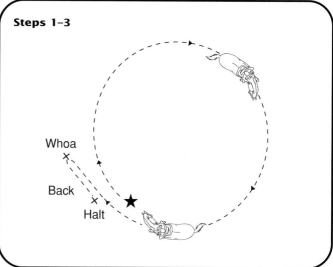

Step 2

3. Back him up two steps, and halt. Feel the horse "stand up," or raise his hindquarters back into a normal position.

4. Walk the horse again in a large circle. When you approach the spot where you stopped last time, test the horse by saying "whoa."

Look for the stop — do you feel him drop his hindquarters? Touch the rein to feel the give.

5. Turn to circle in the other direction, and repeat the "whoa" on two circles. When your horse responds well at the walk, try the command at the trot.

6. Trot in a large circle.

7. Say "whoa" and rock back. Do you feel a difference in the way your horse stops?

8. Lope in a large circle.

9. Stop from the lope at the same place three times. On the third time, you should feel him ready for the cue.

Tips

■ Make your cue consistent. Every time you tell your horse "whoa," back him up.

■ Look for the horse to stop relaxed, with his head flat.

■ After you say "whoa," give the horse about 8 seconds to stop and back up. If he ignores your cue, then take hold of the reins.

Horse Sense

■ Avoid jerking or throwing your body in the saddle.

■ Don't teach your horse to stop by pulling on him. Teach him to stop at your voice and cue to back up.

 Focus on Form

Your horse should break at the loin, dropping his hindquarters to the ground. You sit deep in the saddle. You lower your hips, while your upper body may raise. Keep your leg down in your heel and foot. You may raise your hands slightly so the horse doesn't pull you forward.

Whirling Walk

You've seen reining horses spin so fast that mane and tail fly. Slow down the action, and you've got a walking spin. California trainer Art Gaytan explains how to transform the turn on the haunches into a full turn — or two, three, or four turns in sequence. You create impulsion by moving your horse with your legs. You should feel him "sit down," with his forehand slightly elevated so he can walk the turn.

Objectives
- To do a turnaround at the walk in one smooth motion
- To walk your horse in a 360-degree turn
- To turn the horse in a smooth and even movement

Benefits
- You will relax the neck and shoulder so the body will follow.
- The 360-degree turn at the walk will help prepare you for the faster turnaround, or spin.

Step, step, step to walk in a turn on the haunches.

Time Frame — Short

Step-by-Step

1. Walk your horse to a spot away from the rail.

2. Halt, and feel the horse shift his weight back on the hindquarters.

3. Press your outside (right) calf to drive the horse into a turn on the haunches to the left, while you lay the right rein on the neck. You should feel the horse cross over its inside front foot with the outside front foot. ▼

Step 3

4. Press again so the horse continues turning left, arcing to the left.

5. Reward the horse. Halt and let him settle while you relax.

6. Walk forward on a loose rein on a large circle.

7. Repeat the maneuver, again to the left. This time, **drop your left hip.** Feel that your hip leans out over the horse's inside hip. ▼

Step 7

Challenge

Combine the turn with the use of the neck rein. Do one full (360-degree) turn to the left. Halt and pet. Walk forward ten strides. Do one full turn to the right. Walk forward ten strides and halt.

8. Try the 360-degree turn to the right.
Reverse your cues. Which way did your horse feel more responsive? Next time you try this maneuver, increase your demand by first asking for a 1½ turn in your horse's weaker direction. ▼

Step 8

Tips

▪ In the ideal spin, the horse will plant his hind end and work off the pivot foot. Don't expect your horse to do this at first.

▪ When you start the arc, your horse will probably "run out" with the hindquarters. Reverse the arc to push him into a pivot on the inside hind leg. The reverse arc of head and neck controls that hind leg.

Horse Sense

▪ Your horse might resist turning by backing up, or locking up, or refusing to complete the turn. Use your outside leg to keep the horse in motion. An active leg prevents any slowdown.

▪ Don't let your horse walk out of the turn. Always halt and let him settle.

▪ Don't demand too many turns in one session, or you can sour your horse. Usually three or four turns will be enough.

▪ You shouldn't have to hold your horse back. He should wait and rest.

Chapter 5 Summary

In this chapter, you asked your horse to carry more weight on the hindquarters. You expected energy and impulsion in these lessons.

▪ How did your horse respond to your requests?
▪ Where did you encounter difficulty?

You may feel unsure that your horse moves with impulsion. Have a helper make a video of you, and study the tape to see how far forward your horse reaches with his hind legs. Look at the cantle of your saddle — does the hind hoof nearest you reach under the horse to that distance? You probably won't be able to change your horse's movement dramatically, but these lessons should help you see some improvement in gait.

Using this knowledge, you'll progress to chapter 6. The next lessons help you to examine how your horse moves forward, straight and true.

Combine your practice in rhythm and impulsion to guide your horse straight forward on a loose rein.

chapter 6

Straightness

You've practiced riding straight lines in previous lessons, but do you and your horse remain consistently straight? This chapter helps you become aware of straightness and presents ways to check that every stride remains forward.

As a rider, your goal is for your horse to move determinedly forward with his spine straight. You guide him between the reins so his legs walk, jog, and lope on the invisible track you visualize.

The horse responds by tracking straight, without wavering. He keeps his shoulders right in front of your hips. His energy propels you forward from back to front, with front and hind feet landing on the same track.

Left on their own, horses tend to drift, instead of moving straight and true. You counteract this tendency by not allowing your horse to move in his own direction. In Western riding, your challenge is to guide your horse on track without constant rein contact.

Straightness also involves an even, level movement. The horse raises knees and hocks to the same level. His ears remain even, without one higher than the other. You'll find that your horse can lean, usually seen as dropping the shoulder. He is also more likely to be stiffer on one side than the other. When he moves unevenly, he isn't completely balanced. His body movement affects his ability to turn.

Horses also adopt ways of going as influenced by their riders. You may have allowed your horse to drift or lean, without being aware of what was happening. If any part of your body is crooked or stiff, your body movement will guide the horse in a less-than-correct response. Your hands should be symmetrical. Your hips should be on the same level, neither one forward of the other.

Riding two-handed, you practice more use of the inside and outside reins. Yet when you return to one-handed, the position challenges you to sit square and centered in the saddle. You may have to remind yourself to crank your waist slightly to the left, as you hold the reins in your left hand. And in that position, you mentally check that your shoulders remain square and even.

Lessons in this chapter help you check the position of both you and your horse. You'll also practice the advanced lateral exercises of shoulder-in and two-track, which help you encourage straightness along with impulsion. While maintaining energy and obedience, both you and your horse track straight at any gait.

Toothpaste Tube

Pressing hard on the end of a toothpaste tube makes the paste spurt straight out. When you lope, aim to emulate the paste's path. Your legs tell the horse to lope on a straight line. Horses tend to drift, even if you stay far from the in-gate, and you'll rely on your eye and leg to stay on course. Think about your horse's following his nose in a straight line, without wavering or weaving.

Objectives

- To reinforce the horse's loping in a straight line
- To practice guiding your horse straight, using your eyes to focus and your aids to steer

Ride in a straight line at any gait. Focus on the direction you plan to travel.

- To counteract your horse's tendency to drift in a certain direction

Benefits

- Your horse will tend to go where you look.
- You will dictate a straight line at the lope.

Time Frame — Short

Setup

A pen or arena with a gate on one side. Arrange two cones, as shown opposite. Space them according to the size of your pen.

Step-by-Step

1. Walk your horse down a line of your pen, away from the gate and not immediately beside a fence or a wall. Visualize a line parallel to the fence or wall, on your left.

2. Pick up the lope on the left lead.

3. **Look at the cone. Lope your horse straight to Cone 1.** ▼

Step 3

4. Look where you're going. Remain aware of the line you're loping parallel to, as your focal point. If your horse veers closer to or farther from the line, move him back on the straight line by squeezing with both legs.

Think of your horse like a tube of toothpaste. If you press firmly, the toothpaste shoots out in a straight line.

Some horses may respond better if you push the hip over while loping. Practice what works best with your horse.

5. Halt.

6. Walk a half-circle, so you're lined up to lope to Cone 2. This line places you closer to the gate.

7. Pick up the lope on the right lead. Be ready for your horse to drift toward the gate. Plan to steer him straight. If your horse still drifts away from Cone 2, sidepass him back over to the cone. You're teaching him to listen to your support leg and to stay on the track you set. ▶

8. Halt.

Horse Sense

Guide your horse softly with the reins. Avoid over-steering or overcorrecting your horse.

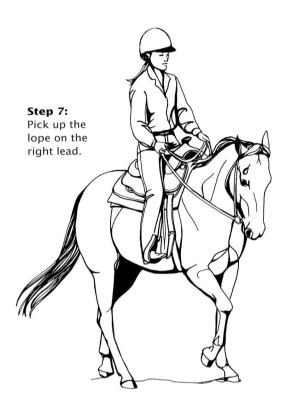

Step 7:
Pick up the lope on the right lead.

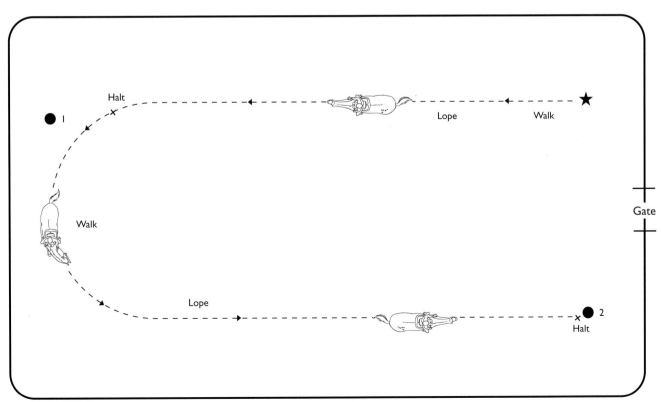

Albuquerque Jerky

Pole benders gallop through six poles. When you do the Jerky, you'll walk, back, half-turn, and sidepass — all with only your neck rein. This lesson tests your horse's ability and willingness to change from straight to curved lines, and from longitudinal to lateral movements. More important, self-test yourself for any uneven aid or crooked position. How can your horse track straight when you're out of alignment?

Objectives
- To test that your horse turns the same, left and right
- To recognize the differences between your horse's left and right sides when bending
- To adjust the intensity of your cues to use both legs and reins the same

Benefit — Your horse will turn more evenly.

Time Frame — Medium

You and your horse influence each other. Sit straight and level to help your horse.

Setup

You'll need five cones or barrels, and four poles. Arrange four cones in a line, 15 feet (4.5 m) apart.

Place the poles to form a lane, as shown below, with the fifth cone at the end. Be ready to ride your horse one-handed through the line.

Step-by-Step

Weaving

1. Halt your horse to line up with Cone 1, one stride away from it.

2. Pick up the walk, bending your horse to walk to the left of Cone 1.

3. Arc the horse to the right.

4. Walk two strides in a straight line.

5. Arc the horse left around Cone 2.

6. Walk two strides in a straight line.

7. Arc the horse right around Cone 3.

8. Walk two strides in a straight line.

9. Arc the horse left around Cone 4.

10. Halt. Ask yourself which of the arcs was easier, to the right or to the left? Did your horse feel stiffer bending in one direction?

11. Walk a half-circle, and repeat the exercise in the opposite direction. Pay attention to your signals. Are they the same weaving right and left?

12. Halt with your right stirrup next to Cone 1.

Challenge

Jog through the "Weaving" segment.

Focus on Form

Your upper body shouldn't change position as you cue the horse. When you shift leg pressure, how far do you lean?

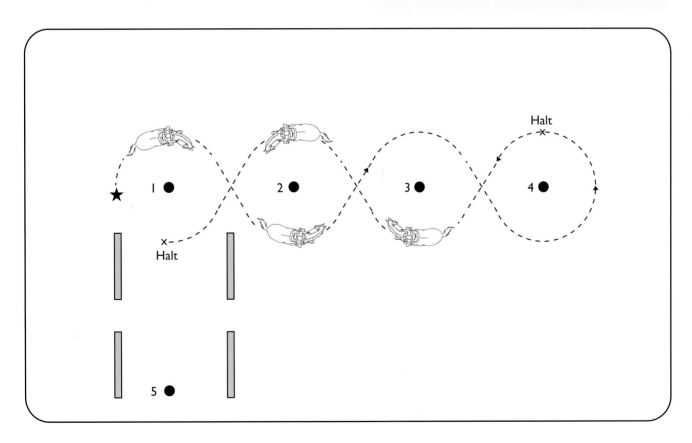

Forward and Back

1. Do a quarter-turn on the haunches so you're lined up with the lane.

2. Walk your horse exactly down the center of the lane.

3. At the end, walk a tight circle to the left around Cone 5. Your stirrup should be no more than 3 feet (1 m) from the cone.

4. Halt with your horse's tail at **x**.

5. Walk one step left in the beginning of a turn on the haunches. Your horse should be facing away from the lane.

6. Back your horse through the lane.

7. Halt when his tail is at Cone 1. How straight did your horse back? Did his hoof-prints follow the same path backing up as they made walking forward?

8. Do a half-turn on the haunches, so your horse stands with his head facing Cone 1.

9. Back your horse through the lane.

10. Halt when his tail is at Cone 5.

11. Sidepass to the right so your horse faces Cone 2.

12. Walk down beside the lane. Maintain an equal distance from the poles at every step.

13. Halt at Cone 2.

Tips

- To be straight, you sit straight and move your limbs equally.
- Do you use your right and left legs the same way? Do your legs remain quiet and still when they should be?
- What about your use of the reins? Do you cue the same when neck reining right and left? Does your hand position change, especially when you rein to the right?

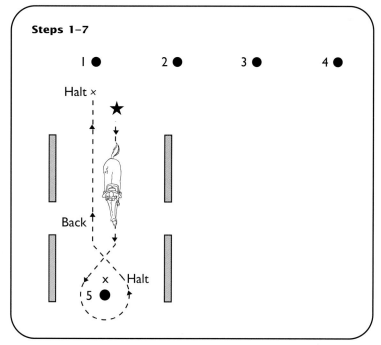

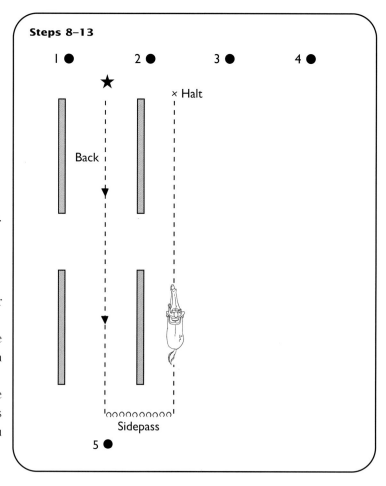

lesson 33

Forward, Sideways, Back

The shoulder-in is a basic suppling exercise, borrowed from the dressage discipline. It expands your control and helps you discriminate between forward lines and lateral tracking. You'll need a helper to tell you when you're truly moving on the "three tracks," as shown on page 127. Besides achieving the position, you'll need to keep your horse going forward in a regular rhythm and impulsion.

Left fore and right hind walk on one track. Right fore and left hind walk on their own tracks.

Objectives

- To encourage the horse to track straight by combining straight lines with the shoulder-in exercise
- To move the horse's inside shoulder off the track, and move it back to the track
- To recognize the feel of riding a straight line without deviation
- To guide the horse with diagonal cues of outside rein, inside leg

Benefits

- This lateral exercise will help supple the horse.
- The horse will learn to maintain a straight line on his own.
- You will test the horse's response to the outside rein.
- The shoulder-in will help the horse carry more weight on the hindquarters.

Time Frame — Medium

Setup

An area with a focal point, such as a post, tree, or cone. (You will be examining your tracks, so try this on ground that's soft or damp.)

Step-by-Step

Shoulder-In on Rail

1. Pick a focal point, at least 60 feet (20 m) from where you plan to start. The point should be down the fence line, but not right beside it. Focus your eyes on that marker.

2. Walk your horse six strides toward the focal point. Halt. Did you feel that you tracked a straight line? Look behind your horse to see the tracks.

3. Resume the walk on a straight line for six more strides.

4. Ask your horse to leg yield to the left, pushing him off your right leg.

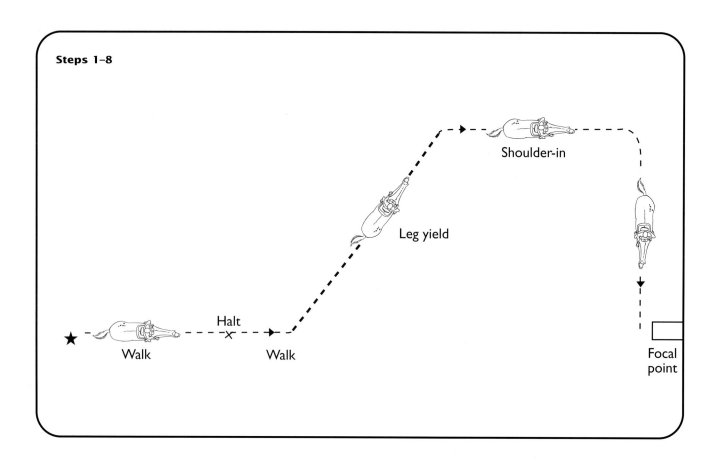

Shoulder-in

Leg yield

Halt

Walk

Walk

Focal point

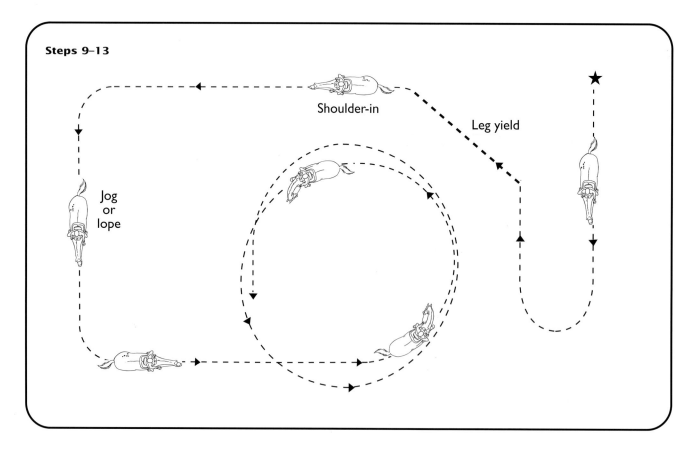

Shoulder-in

Leg yield

Jog or lope

5. At the rail, turn right and walk two strides on a straight line.

6. Begin the shoulder-in, with the horse still responsive to your leg. **Press your inside (right) leg, back of the cinch.** Your inside leg pushes, while the outside leg applies light pressure. **Hold the left (outside) rein on the horse's neck** as an indirect rein to push the shoulders off the rail.

Look for a slight bend, yet a straight neck as you "hold" the shoulder to the inside. Lightly feel contact with the inside rein.

Do you feel the horse's lateral movement? Ask a helper to stand directly behind you and tell you whether your horse is walking on three tracks, with a slight bend. ▼

7. At first, **ask for only four or five strides at the shoulder-in.** Soften your cues and squeeze with both legs for a normal, straight walk. You should feel a definite difference between the lateral and forward directions. ▼

Step 7

8. Walk around the corner and head toward the focal point.

9. Walk a half-circle, so you walk to the right.

Challenge

Try the shoulder-in at the jog, first on the rail and then in the pen.

Step 6

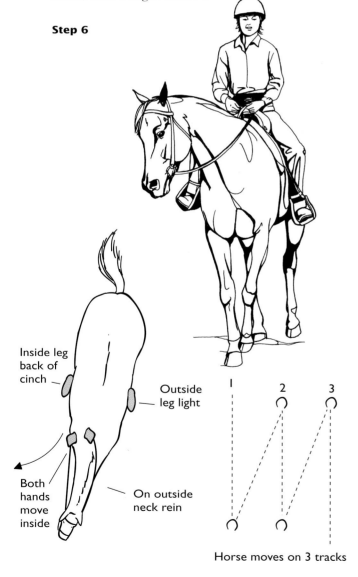

Inside leg back of cinch

Outside leg light

Both hands move inside

On outside neck rein

I   2   3

Horse moves on 3 tracks

10. Leg yield to the rail. ▼

Step 10

11. Repeat the shoulder-in along the rail in this direction.

12. Walk straight. Turn to the left.

13. Jog or lope your horse down the center of the pen, jog to the left, and then do two large circles. Follow the demands of slow, lateral work with free forward movement.

Shoulder-In Solo

1. Move into the pen, away from the rail.

2. Ask for a shoulder-in to the right.

3. Keep walking on the straight line, sustaining the bend in the forward movement.

4. After six strides that feel correct, continue walking forward on a straight line.

Tips

• Haunches stay on the rail or in a straight line in the shoulder-in.
• Keep your horse connected to the outside rein through contact.
• Look for the inside eye.
• Sit tall as you feel the horse "wrapped around" your inside leg, and how he carries the maneuver on the hindquarters.

Horse Sense

• Don't pull with the inside rein. Keep the neck straight.
• The horse shouldn't "break" at the shoulder. Look for a smooth, slight bend.
• Don't let the hindquarters swing out. Your legs keep the horse in position.

lesson 34

Two-Track

When you've practiced the leg yield (see lesson 25 on page 98), the two-track will seem similar. However, the two movements differ in difficulty. In the two-track (called the half-pass in dressage), your horse bends inside, toward the direction he's moving. Horses that readily accept the leg yield may slip back into the easier position of the neck bent away from the direction of travel. A correct two-track demands concentration and practice.

Objectives

- To develop your horse's flexibility, impulsion, and collection
- To walk and jog your horse in the two-track movement
- To keep your horse's spine straight, going forward and laterally

Benefits

- The two-track will help your horse go straight, with a distinction between straight forward and laterally forward.
- Lateral flexibility will help supple your horse. He will be more maneuverable so he's ready for the demands of the trail class, horsemanship, and reining. The maneuver will help his lead changes and turnarounds because he crosses over in front.
- In the show pen, using this movement to pass another horse will display finesse.

Lateral work will help the horse move from back to front. You will build his strength so he can reach under himself.

Time Frame — Medium

Setup

A pen. In "Passing Zone" variation, place two cones 40 feet (12 m) apart.

Step-by-Step

1. Tracking to the right, walk your horse along the rail.

2. Ask for a shoulder-in as you near the corner.

You're asking your horse for a difficult movement. Realize the extent of the challenge and reward his attention and improvement.

3. Walk around the corner in shoulder-in. ▼

4. Continue using your left (outside) indirect rein to push the horse over. **Increase your left leg pressure behind the cinch to move the horse off the rail** (**A**). Your inside leg at the cinch keeps urging the horse to walk forward, and your weight shifts to your inside (right) seatbone. **Feel your inside rein (as a direct rein) to help the horse bend slightly toward the direction he's moving** (**B**).

The horse should feel as if he's moving on two tracks, at a 45-degree angle. His outside fore and outside hind legs cross over in front of the inside legs. ▼

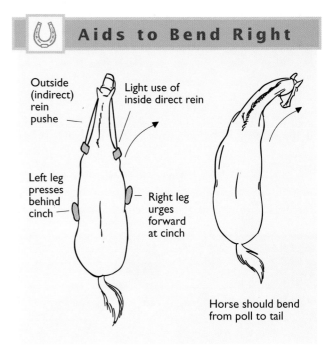

Aids to Bend Right

Outside (indirect) rein pushe

Light use of inside direct rein

Left leg presses behind cinch

Right leg urges forward at cinch

Horse should bend from poll to tail

Step 3:
Walk around the corner in shoulder-in.

Step 4:
Increase your left leg pressure behind the cinch.

Step 4:
Feel your inside rein to help the horse bend slightly toward the direction he's moving.

A   B

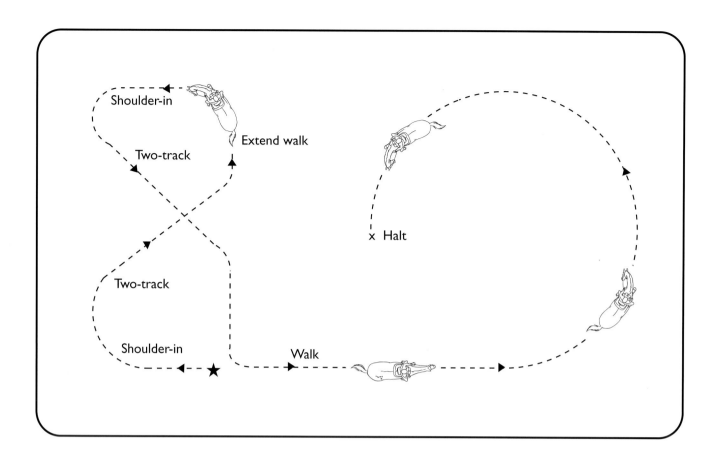

5. At first, ask for only two or three strides at the two-track. Let your horse walk straight on the diagonal, across the pen, and pet him for trying.

6. Move your horse into an extended walk.

7. Turn left, and shorten the walk to prepare for the two-track to the left.

8. Ride your horse in shoulder-in to the left, around the corner.

9. Continue using your right (outside) indirect rein. Increase your right leg pressure behind the cinch to move the horse off the rail. Urge him forward with your inside leg, and feel the inside rein for the bend.

10. Again, stop your cues after you feel the horse try the movement for two or three strides. Pet him as you freely walk across the pen.

Tips

- Understand how the two-track differs from the leg yield. This exercise places greater demands on the horse.
- Feel how the nose, shoulder, and rib cage give to your signals, as you go forward and to the side. Push harder with the outside leg for the crossover.
- Keep the bend to the inside, as you move from shoulder-in to two-track. Ideally the horse's body remains straight, parallel with the fence line, with the neck bent. The head leans slightly in the direction of movement.
- Keep your inside shoulder back and your outside shoulder slightly forward.
- When passing another horse, you must calculate the distance and speed. Know when to begin your two-track, how far to jog past, and when to return to the rail.

Passing Zone

1. Tracking right, jog your horse along the rail toward Cone 1.

2. At Cone 1, **ask for the two-track.** Move your horse off the rail for three strides. ▼

Step 2

3. Jog straight for eight strides. You are passing an imaginary horse. Look ahead at Cone 2.

4. Two-track back to the rail, aiming to return to the straight line at Cone 2. Repeat this exercise with another horse on the rail. You will pass the slower horse without increasing your speed.

Horse Sense

▪ You'll lose impulsion when you first start the two-track. Keep pushing with your outside leg. Moving into this movement from shoulder-in helps keep the horse moving actively.

▪ Realize that this is a difficult exercise for the horse. If it's new to him, ask for only a few strides at a time.

Challenge

Try the two-track at the jog — only after you can perform it at the walk for at least six strides in each direction.

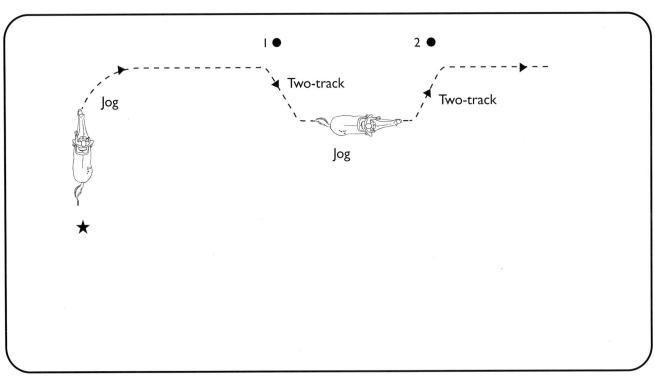

Connected to the Horse

In this final lesson, New Mexico trainer Carolyn Bader explains the basics of collection. You want the horse to carry himself straight forward on his own, whether he has compressed or lengthened his body. Collection helps him use himself, so he's able to rebalance after transitions. This exercise also tests how well your horse understands your leg and hand.

Objectives

- To lengthen the stride to the length of the horse's leg or body, and to shorten the stride
- To adjust your horse's pace and evaluate his response
- To recognize the differences between collected and lengthened gaits
- To control your body as you sit with the horse's motion

Benefit

The horse will maintain rhythm and cadence as he shortens and lengthens.

Time Frame — Medium

Setup

Arrange four cones 10 feet (3 m) from the pen's corners, as shown on page 135.

Stop your body movement in a "half circle" to ask your horse to collect.

Step-by-Step

1. From Cone 1, walk the horse in a straight line for four strides. Feel the rhythm of your horse's normal walk.

2. Ask the horse to lengthen the walk. Squeeze with your calves. You can also bump your horse's sides with your heels or lower legs.

Deepen your seat to get the impulsion forward. Your hips push forward to follow the motion of his back.

Use more leg and constant effort to push your horse forward. ▼

Step 2

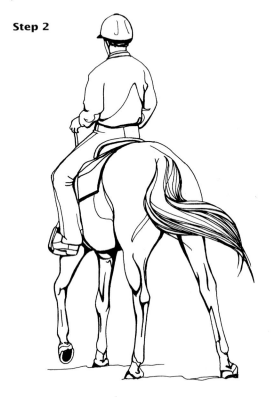

3. As you turn around Cone 2, **slow the walk and ask the horse to collect.** Close your fingers, stop your body movement in hips and legs, and think, "shorter, shorter." Sit deep in the saddle and feel the rhythm of the hind legs.

Can you feel how the horse moves with hocks under him, supporting his weight while propelling himself forward? ▶

4. At Cone 3, ask for another lengthened walk.

5. At Cone 4, again collect the walk.

6. Turn the horse left after Cone 4, to walk diagonally across to Cone 2. Drop the reins and feel how your horse responds when you sit without cueing him.

You're testing each stride for how he propels himself forward. Can you feel the impulsion forward? Does he lose or maintain his energy?

7. Turn left at Cone 2, and pick up the jog. Aim for a relaxed, slow trot. Does the horse jog with energy, lazily, or hurriedly?

8. At Cone 3, ask the horse to lengthen the jog into a trot. Does he respond at once, lag behind, or surge ahead? If the horse is lazy, push him with your legs. If he trots too fast, don't restrain him. Push him so he reaches farther forward with the hind legs, and make him work harder.

9. Slow to the jog as you approach Cone 4.

10. Circle Cone 4 at the jog.

11. Jog to Cone 1.

Step 3: Slow the walk and ask your horse to collect.

Steps 1–6

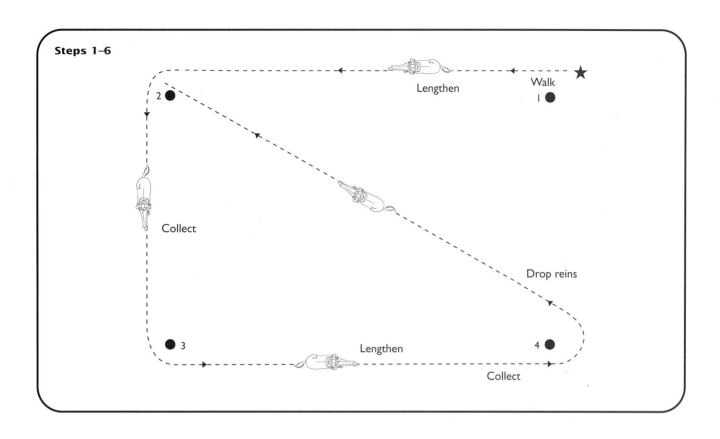

Lengthen

Walk

I ●

2 ●

Collect

Drop reins

● 3

Lengthen

4 ●

Collect

Steps 7–11

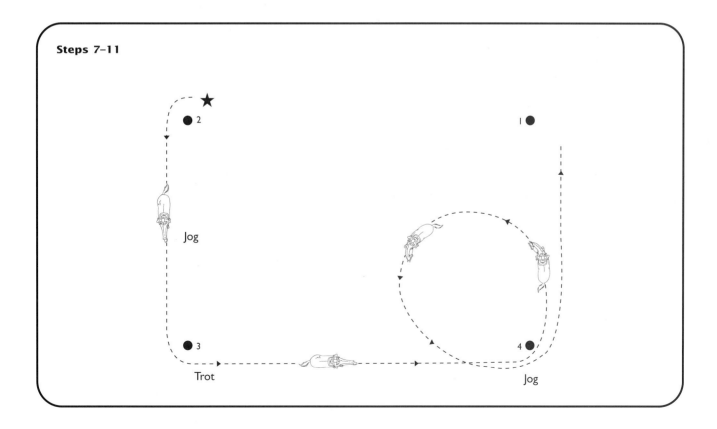

● 2

I ●

Jog

● 3

4 ●

Trot

Jog

12. Turn wide around Cone 1, and pick up the lope on the left lead. Before you ask for the lope, think about your horse's attitude. Does he feel lively today, or is he lazy?

13. Lope toward Cone 3.

14. Change leads two-thirds of the way across the pen, on the diagonal.

15. Stay in the slow lope after the change. Turn right around Cone 3.

16. Lope toward Cone 2.

17. Turn right around Cone 2.

18. Ask your horse to shift gears, **extending into a faster lope across the pen.** ▶

19. Slow the lope as you near Cone 4.

20. Halt at Cone 4.

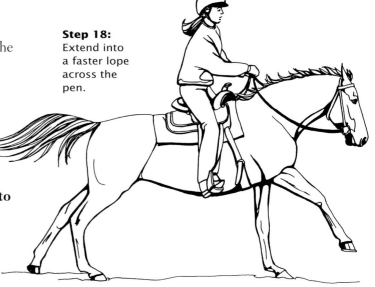

Step 18: Extend into a faster lope across the pen.

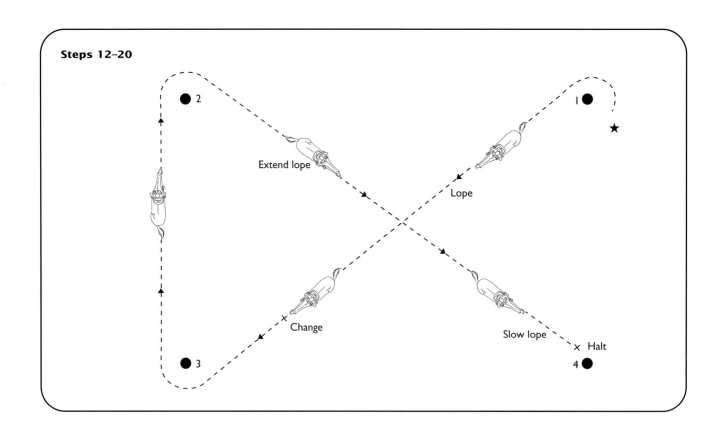

Steps 12–20

2

1

★

Extend lope

Lope

× Change

3

Slow lope

× Halt

4

Tips

- Your horse should feel as if he's driving his body forward to his face.
- Continue assessing his attitude at each upward transition.
- If your horse doesn't respond readily to your cues to lengthen, you may need to wear spurs.

Horse Sense

- Avoid being sudden in your rein movement.
- The horse shouldn't feel as if he's pulling you out of the saddle.

- Don't try to pull a horse into collection or restrict forward motion in a severe manner. Pulling on the head and making it lower doesn't help the horse carry his back and his hocks under him.

Challenge

Try this exercise out of your regular riding area. You can practice lengthening and collecting each gait on a path or in a field. If you ride in an area with bushes or trees, pick certain plants to use as your markers.

Chapter 6 Summary

Your horse should now feel more "broke." He should move in balance, from back to front, without jostling you.

Watch your horse on video to check that he truly maintains straightness. Check his gaits by observing whether his knees and hocks are level. If he has a lot of "chrome" (high white markings), don't let the color difference deceive you from evaluating the quality of his gaits.

By progressing to the end of this chapter, you and your horse have worked hard through this series. You're now on your way to being a good hand. Along the way, you've identified any gaps in your horse's education. If he doesn't respond readily to any particular cue, you know how to adjust your signals. You know the amount of leg you need to apply and the amount of pressure you need to overcome his level of resistance. When you pick up the reins, you can predict the amount of cushion in your horse's mouth.

In your schooling, remember to keep the ideal performance in your mind, without demanding that your horse perform every maneuver perfectly. Look for a genuine effort so you sustain your horse's desire to work. When he tries to please you, you'll both enjoy your lessons.

You can extend the lessons in this book by trying others. Practice the tests published in association rule books, such as horsemanship tests and reining patterns. Attend clinics presented by experts, and watch the best riders school at horse shows. If you closely observe a master, you can learn new approaches and techniques to apply to your own riding.

With horse, saddlery, and outfit, you celebrate the tradition of the Western riding sport.

appendixes

The Western Horse

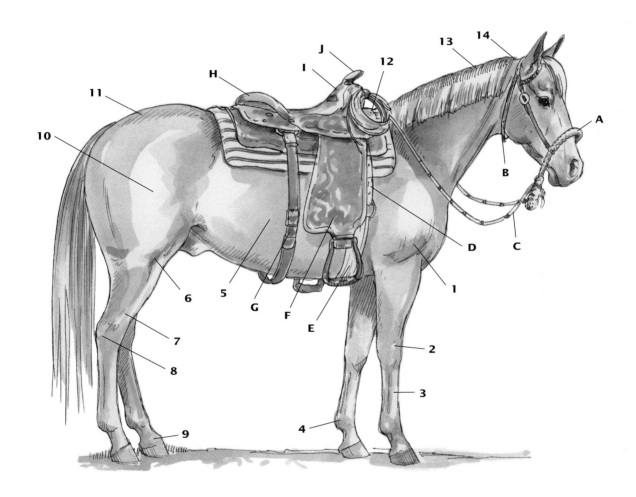

Tack Components

A Bosal
B Throatlatch
C Mecate
D Billet (also called "latigo")
E Cinch
F Fender
G Flank billet
H Cantle
I Pommel
J Horn

Anatomy

1 Shoulder
2 Knee
3 Cannon bones
4 Fetlock
5 Barrel
6 Stifle
7 Gaskin
8 Point of hock
9 Pastern
10 Hindquarters
11 Croup
12 Withers
13 Crest
14 Poll

Further Reading

General

Burns, Deborah, ed. *Storey's Horse-Lover's Encyclopedia*. North Adams, MA: Storey Publishing, 2001.

Foreman, Monte, and Patrick Wyse. *Monte Foreman's Horse-Training Science*. Norman, OK: University of Oklahoma, 1983.

Forget, J.P. *The Complete Guide to Western Horsemanship*. Hoboken, NJ: Howell House Books, 1995.

Hill, Cherry. *Becoming an Effective Rider*. North Adams, MA: Storey Publishing, 1991.

Jones, Suzanne Norton. *Art of Western Riding*. North Hollywood, CA: Wilshire, 1992.

Kirksmith, Tommie. *Ride Western Style*. Hoboken, NJ: Howell House Books, 1991.

————. *Western Performance: A Guide for Young Riders*. Hoboken, NJ: Howell House Books, 1993.

Mayhew, Bob. *Art of Western Riding*. Hoboken, NJ: Howell House Books, 1990.

Smith, Mike. *Getting the Most from Riding Lessons*. North Adams, MA: Storey Publishing, 1998.

Strickland, Charlene. *Show Grooming: The Look of a Winner*, second edition. Emmaus, PA: Breakthrough, 1995.

————. *Tack Buyers Guide*. Emaus, PA: Breakthrough, 1988.

Tellington-Jones, Linda, and Ursula Bruns. *Introduction to the Tellington-Jones Equine Awareness Method*. Emmaus, PA: Breakthrough, 1988.

Specific Western Disciplines

Carpenter, Doug. *Western Pleasure: Training and Showing to Win*. Austin, TX: EquiMedia, 1995.

Dunning, Al. *Reining*. Colorado Springs, CO: Western Horseman, 1998.

Hill, Cherry. *Advanced Western Exercises*. North Adams, MA: Storey Publishing, 1998.

————. *Beginning Western Exercises*. North Adams, MA: Storey Publishing, 1998.

————. *Intermediate Western Exercises*. North Adams, MA: Storey Publishing, 1998.

Livingston, Phil. *Team Penning*. Colorado Springs, CO: Western Horseman, 1991.

Loomis, Bob. Reining: *The Art of Performance in Horses*. Austin, TX: EquiMedia, 1994.

Loving, Nancy. *Go the Distance*. North Pomfret, VT: Trafalgar Square, 1998.

Shrake, Richard. *Western Horsemanship*. Colorado Springs, CO: Western Horseman, 1987.

Strickland, Charlene. *The Basics of Western Riding*. North Adams, MA: Storey Publishing, 1998.

————. *Competing in Western Shows and Events*. North Adams, MA: Storey Publishing, 1998.

Associations

Breed Associations

American Buckskin Registry Association
1141 Hartnell Avenue
Redding, CA 96002-2113
530-223-1420
www.americanbuckskin.com

American Morgan Horse Association
122 Bostwick Road
Shelburne, VT 05482
802-985-4944
www.morganhorse.com

American Paint Horse Association
P.O. Box 961023
Fort Worth, TX 76161-0023
817-834-2742
www.apha.com

American Quarter Horse Association
P.O. Box 200
Amarillo, TX 79168
806-376-4811
www.aqha.com

Appaloosa Horse Club
2720 West Pullman Road
Moscow, ID 83843
208-882-5578
www.appaloosa.com

International Arabian Horse Association
10805 East Bethany Drive
Aurora, CO 80014
303-696-4500
www.iaha.com

International Buckskin Horse Association, Inc.
P.O. Box 268
Shelby, IN 46377
219-552-1013
www.ibha.com

National Quarter Pony Association, Inc.
3232 US 42 South
Delaware, OH 43015
www.nqpa.com

Palomino Horse Breeders of America, Inc.
15253 E. Skelly Drive
Tulsa, OK 74116-2637
918-438-1234
www.palominohba.com

Pinto Horse Association of America, Inc.
7330 NW 23rd Street
Bethany, OK 73008
405-491-0111
www.pinto.org

Pony of the Americas Club, Inc.
5240 Elmwood Avenue
Indianapolis, IN 46203
317-788-0107
www.poac.org

Show/Contest Associations

National Barrel Horse Association
725 Broad Street
Augusta, GA 30901-1050
706-722-7223
www.nbha.com

National Cutting Horse Association
260 Bailey Avenue
Fort Worth, TX 76107-1862
817-244-6188
www.nchacutting.com

National Reining Horse Association
3000 NW 10th Street
Oklahoma City, OK 73107
405-946-7400
www.nrha.com

Glossary

Alternate leg. Pressure of one calf, then the other, in rhythm with the horse's forelegs

Arc. The curvature of the horse's body, bent in the utmost lateral flexion

Bend. To curve easily from poll to tail

Broke. A finished horse, completely trained

Bump. To pull and release the reins for a brief contact with the horse's mouth

Cadence. A balanced, rhythmic sequence of footfalls, with plenty of "air time," or suspension

Collection. Coordinating the horse's moving forward with impulsion, while shortening the body

Counter canter. Purposefully loping on the outside lead rather than the inside lead

Direct rein. Rein contact that leads the horse toward a specific direction; rein held out to the side

Downward transition. A change to a slower or shortened gait

Engage. To carry the hind legs well under

Face. The front of the horse's head; indicates the poll and mouth

Flex. To bend the horse to the inside; also to give to the poll and yield to rein contact

Forehand. The horse's shoulders and legs

Frame. The side view of the horse's body in motion; an individual stride

Hackamore. Bosal.

Half-circle. A loop, shaped like a horseshoe

Half-seat. Rising up out of the saddle, with weight on the stirrups rather than on the seatbones

Half-turn. A turn of 180 degrees

Hesitate. To check the horse momentarily, using rein and leg contact

Impulsion. Forward energy

Indirect rein. Rein contact that guides the horse from one side to the other; rein laid on the neck or above the withers

Inside. In a pen, the side of the horse toward the center

Lateral. Running sideways

Leg yield. A lateral movement, with the horse moving forward and sideways; the horse looks away from the direction he is going

Lock. To freeze up or stiffen

Longitudinal. Running lengthwise

Long trot. An extended jog; a brisk trot

On the forehand. Moving with too much weight on the shoulders and front legs

Outside. In a pen, the side of the horse toward the fence

Overstep. Stepping over the hoofprint of a front foot with the hind foot on the same side

Quarter-turn. A turn of 90 degrees

Rail work. Circling the pen on the fence line

Rollback. A rapid turn of 180 degrees from the trot or the lope, with the horse pivoting on his haunches

Serpentine. A winding pattern of loops, in which the horse changes directions through the pattern

Shoulder-in. A lateral movement, where the horse moves forward with his shoulder to the inside

Sidepass. To move sideways, crossing one leg over another

Strung out. Moving without engaging the hindquarters so the hind end drags behind the forehand

Supple. Bending and flexing willingly to a rider's signals

Track. The line of travel

Turnaround. A full turn of 360 degrees; a spin

Two-track. A lateral movement, where the horse's forefeet and hind feet move on separate tracks; the horse looks where he is going

Upward transition. A change to a faster or lengthened gait

index

Adjust the Brakes, 34–36

"Aha," recognizing, 4

Aids. *See* Leg aids; Rein (hand) aids;
Riding position; Seat aid

Albuquerque Jerky, 122–24

Alternate leg, 15, 142

Arcs, 64–67, 106–8, 142. *See also*
Circles; Serpentines

Arena illustrations key, 5

Associations, 141

ASTM/SEI helmets, 7

Attitude for lessons, 7

Backing up, 34–36

Bader, Carolyn, 37–40, 61–63,
133–37

Balance, 9, 57, 68–70

Bending (flexing), 10–12, 47–49,
61–67, 106–8, 142

Berg, Terry, 81–83

Bits for lessons, 5

Body control of horse, 28–33, 44–46

Body language of horse, 27

Boxed In, 84–87

Break Up the Drive Train, 44–46

Breed associations, 141

Broke horse, 142

Brubaker, Marge, 31–33, 41–43,
74–77, 84–87

Bumping reins, 142

Cadence, 142

Circles, Square-Cornered, 78–80

Circle Up, 47–49

Coiled Mecate, 106–8

Collection, 94–97, 133–37, 142

Connected to the Horse, 133–37

Contest associations, 141

Counter canter, 103–5, 142

Crosswise Loops, 51

Cues, Refine Your, 81–83

Dallas Diagonal, 109–11

"Dead" feeling, 89

Diagonal work, 109–11

Direct rein use, 38, 39, 61–67, 142

Downward transitions, 142. *See also*
Transitions

Drifting and straightness, 119

Energy of horse, 16–18, 25
Engagement of hindquarters, 89,
  90–93, 112–14, 142
Eyes of rider, 68

Face of horse, 142
"Falling on the forehand," 24
Ferguson, Gary, 44–46
Fingertip Controls, 58–60
Flexing, 10–12, 47–49, 61–67,
  106–8, 142
Flying lead change, 78–80
Footfalls and rhythm, 9
Forehand, turn on the, 41–43, 47
Forehand of horse, 142
Forward, Sideways, Back, 125–28
Forward motion, 10–12
Frame, 142

Gait changes. *See* Transitions
Gaytan, Art, 115–17

Hackamore, 142
Half-circles, 68–70, 142
Half-pass, 129–32
Half-seat riding, 94–97, 142
Half-turn, 142
Hand aids. *See* Rein (hand)aids
Haunches, Turn on the, 90–93
Helmets for safety, 7
Hesitation, 142
Hindquarters engagement of, 89,
  90–93, 112–14
  stopping on, 112–14

Hollow back, 33
Horse anatomy, *139*

Idaho Isolation, 41–43
Impulsion, 89–117, 142
  bending (flexing), 106–8
  Coiled Mecate, 106–8
  collection and, 94–97, 142
  Dallas Diagonal, 109–11
  diagonal work, 109–11
  engagement of hindquarters, 89,
    90–93, 112–14, 142
  half-seat riding, 94–97, 142
  Haunches, Turn on the, 90–93
  leg yield, 98–102
  lengthening stride, 109–11
  Outside Rein Rhythm, 94–97
  serpentines, 103–5
  shortening stride, 109–11
  Sidewinder, 98–102
  Snake River Serpentines, 103–5
  speed, varying, 90–93, 103–5,
    109–11
  spinning, 93, 115–17
  Stop on Your Butt, 112–14
  transitions, 94–97, 103–5, 109–11
  turnarounds, 93, 115–17, 143
  Turn on the Haunches, 90–93
  Whirling Walk, 93, 115–17
Indirect rein use, 38, 39, 40, 61–67,
  142
Inside of horse, 142
In Your Corner, 28–30

Jaw, relaxing, 28–33, 57
Jogging rhythm, 9, 16–18

King, Joe, 28–30, 78–80

Laredo Lope, 22–24
Lateral exercises, 142. *See also*
    Shoulder-in; Sidepassing;
    Sidewinder; Two-Track
Leg aids
    for impulsion, 93, 94, 97, 102
    for readiness, 64, 67, 68, 71, 77,
        79, 83
    for relaxation and suppleness, 28,
        31, 36, 43, 46, 47, 49, 55
    for rhythm, 12, 14, 15, 18, 21, 24
    for straightness, 124, 130, 132
Leg yield, 98–102, 142
Lengthening stride, 109–11, 133–37
Lengthwise Loops, 53
Lightness to cues, 27, 34–36
Line through the Lane, 10–12
Location for lessons, 7
Locking up, 142
Longitudinal, 142
Long trotting, 142
Loping, 9, 22–24, 120–21
Loping the Loops, 54–55

Mirrored Hackamore, 68–70

Natural movement (horse), 9
Neck reining, 57, 74–77
Nevada Neck Rein, 74–77

Objectives of lessons, 4
Obstacles, negotiating, 19–21

"Off the bit," 58
One-handed riding, 57, 74–77
"On the aids," 55, 57
"On the forehand," 142
"Opening doors," 46, 63
Outside of horse, 142
Outside Rein Rhythm, 94–97
Outside rein use, 61–67
Overstep, 142

Passing another horse, 129–32
Ponderosa Poles, 19–21

Quarter-turn, 142

Rail work, 142
Readiness, 57–87
    arcs, 64–67, 142
    balance for, 57, 68–70
    bending (flexing), 61–67
    Boxed In, 84–87
    direct rein use, 61–67
    Fingertip Controls, 58–60
    half-circles, 68–70, 142
    indirect rein use, 61–67
    Mirrored Hackamore, 68–70
    neck reining, 57, 74–77
    Nevada Neck Rein, 74–77
    one-handed riding, 57, 74–77
    outside rein use, 61–67
    Refine Your Cues, 81–83
    reverse arcs, 66–67
    reversing, 68–70
    shoulders, keeping up, 78–80
    shoulders, moving with reins,
        61–63

Sidepassing, 71–73, 143
slowing the horse, 78–80
Square-Cornered Circles, 78–80
Stay on Track, 64–67
Striding and Guiding, 61–63
transitions for, 57, 84–87
turns and, 78–80
Refine Your Cues, 81–83
Rein (hand) aids
    for impulsion, 92, 94–97, 102
    for readiness, 58–67, 77, 79, 83
    for relaxation and suppleness, 28,
        31, 37–40, 43, 45, 46, 47, 55
    for rhythm, 12, 14, 18, 21, 24
    for straightness, 121, 124, 128, 130
Relaxation and suppleness, 27–55
    Adjust the Brakes, 34–36
    backing up, 34–36
    bending (flexing), 47–49
    body control of horse, 28–33,
        44–46
    Break Up the Drive Train, 44–46
    Circle Up, 47–49
    Crosswise Loops, 51
    direct rein use, 38, 39
    forehand, turn on the, 41–43, 47
    Idaho Isolation, 41–43
    indirect rein use, 38, 39, 40
    In Your Corner, 28–30
    of jaw, 28–33
    Lengthwise Loops, 53
    lightness to cues, 27, 34–36
    Loping the Loops, 54–55
    Relax the Jaw, 31–33
    Serpentine Circus, 50–55
    shoulders, keeping up, 47–49
    Sittin' and Bittin', 37–40
    Tightened Loops, 52

transitions, 34–36, 50–55
turn on the forehand, 41–43,
    47
yielding to pressure, 28–33,
    44–46
Relax the Jaw, 31–33
Resistance to cues, 5
Reverse arcs, 66–67
Reversing, 68–70
Rhythm, 9–25
    bending, 10–12
    energy of horse, 16–18, 25
    footfalls and, 9
    forward motion, 10–12
    of jogging, 9, 16–18
    Laredo Lope, 22–24
    Line through the Lane, 10–12
    of loping, 9, 22–24
    obstacles and, 19–21
    Ponderosa Poles, 19–21
    Singin' in the Walk, 13–15
    Sit the Jog, 16–18
    on straight line, 10–12
    transitions, 19–24
    of walking, 9, 13–15
Riding position (form)
    for impulsion, 96, 112, 117
    for readiness, 59, 67, 77, 87
    for relaxation and suppleness, 36,
        40, 43, 49, 55
    for rhythm, 12, 14, 17, 18, 21, 24,
        25
    for straightness, 119, 124, 137
Ringside reference tip, 3
Rollback, 143
Round back, 33, 89
Rubbernecking, 63, 67
"Run out" with hindquarters, 117

Safety helmets, 7
Seat aid
    for impulsion, 92, 96, 112
    for readiness, 67
    for relaxation and suppleness, 43,
      45, 55
    for rhythm, 10, 14, 16, 24
Serpentine Circus, 50–55
Serpentines, 103–5, 143
Shortening stride, 109–11, 133–37
Shoulder-in, 125–28, 143
Shoulders of horse
    keeping up, 47–49, 78–80
    moving with reins, 61–63
Show associations, 141
Sidepassing, 71–73, 143
Sidewinder, 98–102
Singin' in the Walk, 13–15
Sit the Jog, 16–18
Sittin' and Bittin', 37–40
Snaffle bit for lessons, 5
Snake River Serpentines, 103–5
Speed, varying, 78–80, 90–93, 103–5,
    109–11
Spinning, 93, 115–17
Spurs, use of, 81–83
Square-Cornered Circles, 78–80
Stay on Track, 64–67
Stop on Your Butt, 112–14
Straight line riding, 10–12
Straightness, 119–37
    Albuquerque Jerky, 122–24
    collection, 133–37, 142
    Connected to the Horse, 133–37
    Forward, Sideways, Back, 125–28
    half-pass, 129–32
    lengthening stride, 133–37

    loping, 120–21
    passing another horse, 129–32
    shortening stride, 133–37
    shoulder-in, 125–28
    Toothpaste Tube, 120–21
    turns and, 122–24
    Two-Track, 129–32, 143
    Weaving, 123
Striding and Guiding, 61–63
"Strung out," 24, 57, 68, 143
"Suck back," 108
Suppleness, 143. *See also* Relaxation
    and suppleness

Tack components, *139*
"Three tracks," 125
Tightened Loops, 52
Time frame for lessons, 4
Toothpaste Tube, 120–21
Top line of horse, 9, 143
Tracking, 143
Trail classes, 19–21
Training scale, 1, 2, 3
Transitions
    impulsion and, 94–97, 103–5,
      109–11
    readiness and, 57, 84–87
    relaxation and suppleness and,
      34–36, 50–55
    rhythm and, 19–24
Turnarounds, 93, 115–17, 143
Turn on the forehand, 41–43, 47
Turn on the Haunches, 90–93
Turns, 78–80, 122–24
Two-handed riding, 5
Two-Track, 129–32, 143

Upward transitions, 143. *See also*
    Transitions

Vernon, Guy, 112–14
    Visualization, 57
    Voice and commands, 17

Walking rhythm, 9, 13–15
    Warm up for lessons, 7
    Weaving, 123

Wegener, Terry, 112–14
Western Riding classes, 19–21
Whip, use of, 34, 36, 73
Whirling Walk, 93, 115–17
"Whoa," 112–14

Yielding to pressure, 28–33, 44–46

Other Storey Titles You Will Enjoy

Easy-Gaited Horses, by Lee Ziegler.
An in-depth guide to working with gaited horses by one of the world's leading expert
the subject. Includes line drawings and diagrams.
256 pages. Paper. ISBN 1-58017-562-7. Hardcover. ISBN 1-58017-563-5.

The Rider's Fitness Program,
by Dianna R. Dennis, John J. McCully, and Paul M. Juris.
A unique, six-week workout routine to help build the strength, endurance, and sk
that will enhance the riding experience.
224 pages. Paper. ISBN 1-58017-542-2.

The Rider's Problem Solver, by Jessica Jahiel.
Answers to problems familiar to riders of all levels and styles from a clinician and e
behavior expert.
384 pages. Paper. ISBN 1-58017-838-3. Hardcover. ISBN 1-58017-839-1.

Storey's Illustrated Guide to 96 Horse Breeds of
North America, by Judith Dutson.
A comprehensive encyclopedia filled with full-color photography and in-dep'
on the 96 horse breeds that call North America home.
416 pages. Paper. ISBN 1-58017-612-7. Hardcover with jacket. ISBN 1-5801

Trail Riding, by Rhonda Hart Poe.
Fundamental instruction and detailed advice on every aspect of preparing
cuting a pleasurable trail ride.
336 pages. Paper. ISBN 1-58017-560-0. Hardcover. ISBN 1-58017-561-9.

These books and other books from Storey Publishing are available
wherever quality books are sold or by calling 1-800-441-5700.
Visit us at *www.storey.com*.